Recipes for
FAT FREE LIVING 2
COOKBOOK

EVERY RECIPE
UNDER 1 GRAM OF FAT
PER SERVING

<u>Recipes for FAT-FREE LIVING COOKBOOK 2</u>

ISBN 0-9636876-8-9
Jyl Steinback
Fat-Free Living, Inc.
15202 North 50th Place
Scottsdale, Arizona 85254
602-996-6300

Recipes for Fat Free Living Cookbook

"Your book is wonderful, what a gift! You're an inspiration to all!"
Terry Branson, Stillwater, OK

"I'm writing to tell you how much I like your Fat Free Living Cookbook. I use it every day!"
Dawn Wilson, Sparks, NV

"On January 31, I was 187 pounds (at 5"4"). I told my husband that his birthday present this year would be me doing everything in my power to lose 10 pounds by his birthday, April 3rd.

I had read an article about cutting fat out of ones daily intake. So instead of counting calories this time I counted grams of fat. I started a daily exercise program, as well. By April 3rd I had lost an amazing 18 pounds! And I was still eating plenty of food, never starved myself, and felt great. After a while I even stopped feeling that I was 'missing out' on the 'good' foods.

Now I'm on a roll. I've gone from squeezing into size 18 pants to wearing size 12 comfortably (I can squeeze into size 10, but would rather be comfortable). I'm at 153 pounds, and still losing! Everyone is amazed at the difference. The funny thing is that no one wants to hear that I am eating right and exercising. They want to hear I'm on some miracle diet, or taking shots, or something else drastic. Doing something so simple means they should be doing it themselves, and they don't want to. Best of luck to you!"
Carol Sue Eklund, Yorba Linda, CA

"Congratulations on your healthy idea. I love the name of your company too! I am purchasing your book over and above "In the Kitchen with Rosie," Oprah's favorite. I am not interested in LOW FAT. I am interested in NO FAT! I wish you the very best! My cholesterol is high so I welcome it with open arms."
Beverly B. Peek

"It's finally here, the book I have been waiting for, the book of a lifetime. I have cut the fat in my diet and so far have lost 50 pounds. I'm someone who has been far all of my life and when I discovered that fat makes you fat my whole world changed. With your help I can lose the last twenty pounds and be thin forever. Thank You! You are making a lot of peoples lives change for the better."
Lynn Roden, Tacoma, WA

This book would not have been possible without all the love and support from all of these wonderful people. Thank you all! I love you all very much and LUCKY ME!

Thank you to all my wonderful sharing fat-free friends for your positive strengths and encouragement. You all made this book 2 possible! Thank you!

Thanks to my wonderful family! Mom and Dad, Betty and Bill Levy, you have given me the upbringing to make it all happen! To believe in myself! The greatest gift a parent can give a child. Thank you for both of you! I love you very much!

Thanks Jacie, you are a wonderful sister, and you are always keeping me on top of the latest fat-free foods. I couldn't do it without you, and definitely appreciate you! Love ya lots!

Thanks Jeff, Diane, and Alex, you are all an inspiration in my life. With lot of goals, dreams and ACTION! Yea you! And I think I'm busy! Love you lots!

Thanks Snooky and Harlan, you two are very special to me and I love you very much!

Babba, You're Great and I love you! Keep on bragging and showing those pictures!

Dale, Janet, Jay, and Julia, we need some more "J's" in our family! I love you all very much!

Mikki, you are one in a million! Thank you! You made this book happen! You shared a lot of time, energy, and wonderful knowledge! You are an extremely special person and I am lucky to have you as my friend! I appreciate you and thank you very much!

Thanks Jamie! You are AWESOME! And I love you very much! You are so special in my world, you are caring, loving, a wonderful person, and an incredible big sister. Lucky Scott to have you; Lucky all of us!

Welcome to the world Scott! You have brought us an abundance of joy and laughter, just with your smiling eyes. Thanks for being part of our world! I love you very much! You and Jamie are a wonderful gift and a perfect miracle!

I love you Gary! You are my best friend, lover, husband and absolutely the most positive blessing in my life! Gary you truly are my soul mate and a wonderful, thoughtful, and loving man! I am lucky, Gary, for having you in my life! Thank you for all of your support, energy and positive reinforcement, and a great business mind (to finalize all of our deals). I couldn't and wouldn't want to do it without YOU! I love you more than life. YOU ARE ONE IN A MILLION! HOW DID I GET SO LUCKY? THANK YOU!

ACKNOWLEDGEMENTS

Thank you Ken and Stephanie Wilbanks for your wonderful friendship! For helping make this book possible! I know this was an extremely busy time for you and you still made time for me! I truly appreciate both of you! Your time, energy and wonderful positive attitudes toward life. Thanks for helping make my dreams come true. I wish you both happiness, health, and success always. Hi Alex, Hi Lauren!

Debra Kohl, M.S., R.D. is a registered dietitian with a master's degree in Nutrition and Dietetics from University of Arizona.

Debra has a consulting firm named Kohl-Marx Counseling which specializes in weight management. Healthy Choices Life Management Program is designed for people who are chronically overweight or have habitual dieting syndrome. The program is based on healthy meal planning and nutrition education for gradual, long-term weight change. If focuses on skill building and boundary setting in all self-care areas via cognitive-behavioral counseling. All facets of the program can be adapted to meet patients special needs.

Debra also consults with patients who have eating disorders, hormone therapy, irritable bowl disorders, diabetes, cardiovascular disease and other symptoms or diseases that require nutrition education. Debra may be reached a 602-266-0324.

Thank you Debra; you played such a wonderful part in my book. Thanks for all the breakdowns of each recipe and the exchanges. Also the wonderful article at the beginning of the book. You did a phenomenal job! I appreciate you!

A special thanks to Bev Keniston who did a beautiful job in editing the entire book. Bev exhibits expertise as a magazine writer and newspaper food columnist. A wonderful job you did! I appreciate you Bev, all of your time and energy. Thanks so much!

And a standing ovation to Mikki Eveloff! You're the greatest Mikki! We'll just have to go on tour together, it's just that simple. You're creative, talented, energetic, positive and totally FAT FREE! MY KIND OF FRIEND! THANK YOU A MILLION!

I also want to thank the many people who purchased my first book and made book number 2 possible. Thank you for all your wonderful letters, phone calls and positive feedback. You are all the GREATEST! Keep on believing in yourselves! You are doing a great job!

Things You Need To Know About Fat Free

Everywhere you look, any way you turn, you encounter THE FAT ISSUE. In every magazine, on every talk show, at every dinner party people are discussing FAT! "How many grams of fat are in this!" "What kind of fat is in that?"

As a registered dietitian specializing in weight management I hear these questions every day and I am constantly amazed at the misinformation that's floating around. I have compiled some of the most popular questions and have provided the answers to help clear up the confusion. I hope it helps.

What should my body fat be?

The average female's percent body fat in the U.S. is approximately 30%.

A healthy range for females is 18 - 25% and for males it is 12 - 16%.

What is the best way to measure body fat?

The the most accurate techniques for measuring body fat are hydrostatic weighing (underwater weighing), electrical impedance, and skinfold measurements using calipers. Underwater weighing is the "gold standard" used by most exercise physiologists but the other methods, when performed by experienced individuals are also widely accepted.

How long does it take to lose one pound of fat?

Theoretically one pound of fat is equal to 3500 calories. Therefore if you decrease your calories by 500 calories per day you should lose approximately one pound of body fat in a week.

Why do women look fatter than men?

Female hormones alter metabolic pathways to favor the storage of body fat. Women store fat more easily than men because of:

-female hormones
-less muscle
-unbalanced diet
-lack of exercise

Fat constitutes more than a quarter of the total body weight of most Americans.

What is the function of fat?

Fat is necessary to:

-provide the body with a storage form of metabolic fuel for energy
-protect and support vital organs (heart, liver, etc.)
-promote normal growth, healthy skin and nerves
-insulate against the cold
-transport fat soluble vitamins
-satiate the appetite

What are the disease risks associated with being fat?

High blood pressure
Diabetes
Breast and endometrial cancer
High blood lipids
Menstrual irregularities
Stroke
Kidney disease
Gall bladder disease
Pulmonary disease
Osteoarthritis
Gout

Do we need some fat in our diets?

Yes. We need about 15 to 20 grams per day.

What is the best kind of fat to use?

Remember a fat is a fat and they all have equal calories (9 calories per gram) but monounsaturated fat is your best choice when a fat is needed. Examples of these fats are olive oil, canola oil and peanut oil. When used in place of saturated fats (fat from animal product, palm and coconut oil) monounsaturated fats have been shown to have a cholesterol lowering affect without lowering high density lipoprotein (HDL) levels. HDLs are the good fats that offer protection against heart disease.
*To help eliminate fat while preparing foods you can use water, broth, wine, or plain and simple fat-free Pam.

Does a high fat diet influence the development of any disease?

Yes, studies over the past decade concluded that there is a correlation between a high fat diet and heart disease, breast, prostate and colon cancer, diabetes, and high blood pressure.

"The single most influential dietary change one can make to lower the risk of these diseases is to reduce intake of foods high in fats and to increase the intake of foods high in complex carbohydrates and fiber." - The Surgeon General's Report on Nutrition and Health (1988)

"It is calculated that, if intake of dietary fat were reduced from the present 40% of total calorie intake to 25%, about 9,000 lives would be saved annually." - National Cancer Institute, "Diet and Health" (1989)

Are fat calories different than carbohydrate and protein calories?

Yes, the way the body metabolizes fat is different from the way it handles other calories. Fat is less expensive. In other words, the body is more efficient at processing fat calories. It takes less calories for the body to convert fat calories to body fat. In fact it only takes 3% of the fat calories we eat to turn the food we eat into body fat while it takes 25% of the carbohydrates and protein calories we eat to do the same.

What is the healthiest way to lose fat?

1. A low fat, low sugar and high fiber diet, low enough in calories so that the body will use its fat stores for energy but not so low that it will use its muscle mass.

2. Aerobic exercise to enhance the body's ability to burn fat.

3. Weight lifting for moderate body building to increase fat-burning muscle mass. Also resistance training with rubber bands and weighted balls.
   Almost no fat is burned during weight lifting but changes occur in the muscle that have long-term effects on the body chemistry. For example there is an increase in muscle mass which leads to a greater need for calories by the body. It also stimulates deep muscle levels so that more muscle gets involved during aerobic exercise.

Can I eat as much as I want as long as it's fat-free?

No. If your body requires 1800 calories to maintain your weight and you eat 2000 calories from carbohydrates and protein, you will still store 200 calories as fat. The luxury of eating a low fat diet is to be able to eat a greater volume of food at a lower calorie level. This means no more starving! However, since fat in the diet provides longer periods of fullness than do carbohydrate and protein, you may need to eat several small meals throughout the day to avoid being hungry.

High fat foods are very dense in calories. For example, one pat of butter has more calories than the baked potato you put it on, depending on the size of the potato.

You can actually eat a full days intake of low fat foods for the same calories as a high fat lunch.

LUNCH: 1 Big Mac, large French fries, large Coke

=

BREAKFAST: 1 bowl of cereal, 1/2 cup skim milk, 4 oz. orange juice

LUNCH: Turkey sandwich, side salad with fat-free dressing, apple, pretzels

DINNER: Grilled chicken breast, 1/2 c. noodles, broccoli, skim milk

SNACK: 3 c. of air popped popcorn

**Note: The mathematics of macronutrients

1 gram of carbohydrate has 4 calories
1 gram of protein has 4 calories
1 gram of alcohol has 7 calories
1 gram of fat has 9 calories

How many meals per day should I eat in order to lose fat?

When we eat less than what the body perceives is enough, the body will hold on to fat to prepare us for the upcoming "famine". However, when we eat enough to provide the body with adequate nutrients it will release the fat for the body to use as energy.

You should eat as many meals as your body tells you to eat. You need to eat when you are hungry and stop when you are satisfied, not full.

Don't worry, you can eat again when you get hungry. By listening to your body you will rarely over or under eat and therefore you will not need to store extra fat.

How do I know what I should eat on a daily basis?

Health agencies such as the American Heart Institute, the American Cancer Society and the American Dietetic Association have developed The Guidelines for Healthy Americans. These guidelines assist people in selecting a healthy meal plan. The Guidelines are printed at the bottom of each food label and are used to calculate the % Daily Values. Suggestions include:

-Limiting your fat intake to less than 20% of your calories. This can be calculated by multiplying the calories that you eat by .20 and dividing that number by 9. This means if you eat 2000 calories you should have no more than 44 grams of fat per day.

-Limiting your cholesterol intake to 300 mg per day.

-Limiting your sodium intake to 2400mg per day.

-Increasing your fiber intake to 25gm per day or more.

These guidelines were also used in developing the new Food Guide Pyramid which replaces the Basic 4 Food Groups. The Pyramid reflects a diet consisting of 55% carbohydrate, 15% protein, and 20% fat. An even lower fat intake is encouraged if tolerated.

How much weight can I expect to lose if a low fat, high fiber diet and start doing aerobic exercise and weight lifting?

The answer varies considerably from person to person. The appropriate rate of weight loss is approximately 1 to 2 pounds per week. Faster weight loss may indicate loss of muscle mass which will eventually cause a drop in your metabolic rate. You may see very little weight change if you are building your muscle mass but your clothes may fit more loosely. This is because muscle weighs more than fat but takes up less space.

By integrating some of the following delicious fat-free recipes into your daily meal plan and adding a variety of fresh fruits and vegetables, whole grains and nonfat dairy products you should feel satisfied, meet your nutrient needs and begin to lose body fat. Adding exercise to your new low-fat way of eating will guide you on your way to a leaner, healthier lifestyle.

By: Debra Kohl, M.S., R.D.
Kohl-Marx Counseling

One last question I am always asked...what cookware do I use and recommend?

The Steinback house uses Ameriware Professional Cookware and we have found it to be terrific! Not only does it allow us to cook without butter and oils which are not allowed in a FAT FREE Lifestyle, but it cleans up so quickly too! It is a perfect fit for those of us who want to cook FAT FREE! So throw away your sprays as FAT FREE is here to stay! For more information about the fabulous cookware you can call (818) 909-9898

Jyl...

FAT-FREE FABULOUS FOODS

Appealing Appetizers

Sensational Soups and Sandwiches

Bravo Breakfast/Brunch

Super Salads

Magnificent Main Courses

Fabulous Fish

Perfect Pasta/Ravenous Rice

Vigorous Vegetables

Delectable Desserts

Desirable Drinks

Microwave Magic

Happy Holiday Menus

APPEALING
APPETIZERS

CRABMEAT DIP WITH ZIP

EASY - DO AHEAD

ingredients: 1 package fat-free flaked crabmeat
1 8 oz. package fat-free cream cheese, softened
1 tbsp. lemon juice
1 tbsp. Worcestershire sauce

directions: Mix all the ingredients well and press into a small bowl.
Chill, unmold and garnish with a sprinkling of paprika (optional).
Serve with fat-free crackers.

Serves: 6

Nutrition per Serving		Exchanges
Calories	77	1 meat
Protein	7 grams	1/2 starch
Carbohydrate	8 grams	
Cholesterol	11 milligrams	
Sodium	537 milligrams	
Dietary Fiber	0 grams	

VEGETABLE DIP WITH ZIP

EASY - DO AHEAD

ingredients:
1/2 tsp. dry mustard
1 cup fat-free mayonnaise
2 tbsp. chili sauce
2 tbsp. lime juice
1 tbsp. minced parsley
3 tbsp. minced sweet pickles
1 tsp. onion powder
1/4 tsp. Tabasco sauce

directions:
Mix 2 tablespoons of mayonnaise with the dry mustard and then add the remaining ingredients. Mix well, refrigerate and serve with fresh cut-up vegetables.

Serves: 4

Nutrition per Serving
Calories	55
Protein	< 1 gram
Carbohydrate	11 grams
Cholesterol	0 milligrams
Sodium	460 milligrams
Dietary Fiber	0 grams

Exchanges
3/4 starch

PEPPER CHEESE DIP
EASY - DO AHEAD

ingredients: 2 cups fat-free Monterey Jack cheese, shredded
2 cups fat-free American cheese, shredded
6 green onions, sliced
2/3 cup chopped red bell pepper
2 tbsp. diced jalapeño peppers

directions: Lightly spray a saucepan with cooking spray.
Melt cheeses in saucepan over medium-low heat,
5 to 10 minutes.
Stir in green onion, red pepper, and peppers.
Serve with fat-free tortilla or pita chips.

Yields: 2 cups

Nutrition per Serving

Calories	109
Protein	15 grams
Carbohydrate	12 grams
Cholesterol	12 milligrams
Sodium	882 milligrams
Dietary Fiber	3 grams

Exchanges

1 milk
1 meat

ARTICHOKE DIP

EASY - DO AHEAD

ingredients:
2 10 oz. packages frozen artichoke hearts
1 cup fat-free mayonnaise
1 cup fat-free Parmesan cheese
6 cloves garlic, minced, or 6 tsp. garlic puree
fat-free Parmesan cheese to taste, on top

directions:
Cook artichokes according to package directions.
Drain and cut artichokes into small pieces.
Blend the artichokes with the mayonnaise, Parmesan cheese, and minced garlic.
Place the mixture in an oven-proof dish and bake for 20 minutes at 350 degrees, or until the mixture is hot and bubbly.
Sprinkle the top with Parmesan cheese to taste.
Serve with fat-free crackers or assorted vegetables.

Serves: 6

Nutrition per Serving

Calories	118
Protein	9 grams
Carbohydrate	22 grams
Cholesterol	0 milligrams
Sodium	491 milligrams
Dietary Fiber	0 grams

Exchanges
1 starch
1 1/2 vegetable

SPINACH DIP

EASY - DO AHEAD

ingredients: 2 10 oz. packages frozen chopped spinach,
thawed and drained well
1 cup fat-free sour cream
1 cup fat-free mayonnaise
1 tsp. garlic powder
1 tsp. onion powder
1 tbsp. lemon juice
1 8 oz. can sliced water chestnuts

directions: Combine spinach with all the other ingredients
and mix well. Refrigerate several hours.
Serve with assorted fresh vegetables or fat-free
crackers.

Serves: 6

Nutrition per Serving		Exchanges
Calories	94	1 starch
Protein	6 grams	1 vegetable
Carbohydrate	18 grams	
Cholesterol	0 milligrams	
Sodium	390 milligrams	
Dietary Fiber	2 grams	

CURRY DIP
EASY - DO AHEAD

ingredients:
1/2 cup fat-free sour cream
1 cup fat-free mayonnaise
1 crushed garlic clove
2 tsp. lemon juice
4 tsp. sugar
1 tbsp. curry powder
1/2 cup finely minced parsley

directions:
Mix all ingredients and chill
Great dip with fresh cut-up vegetables.

Serves: 4

Nutrition per Serving

		Exchanges
Calories	83	1 starch
Protein	2 grams	
Carbohydrate	14 grams	
Cholesterol	0 milligrams	
Sodium	444 milligrams	
Dietary Fiber	1 gram	

HONEY MUSTARD DIP

EASY - DO AHEAD

ingredients:
1/2 cup honey
1/2 cup fat-free Dijon mustard
2 tbsp. teriyaki sauce
2 tsp. grated ginger root
1/2 tsp. hot pepper sauce

directions:
Combine all ingredients and blend well.
Serve with fresh cut-up vegetables.

Yields: 1 cup
Serves: 8

Nutrition per Serving

		Exchanges
Calories	93	1/2 starch
Protein	< 1 gram	1 fruit
Carbohydrate	18 grams	
Cholesterol	0 milligrams	
Sodium	563 milligrams	
Dietary Fiber	< 1 gram	

CRABMEAT DIP

EASY - DO AHEAD

ingredients:
8 oz. fat-free cream cheese
8 oz. fat-free crabmeat
1 cup ketchup
1/4 cup horseradish
dash parsley
fat-free crackers

directions:
Combine ketchup and horseradish in a small bowl and mix well. Set aside
Spread cream cheese on a platter.
Top with crabmeat and then cover with ketchup mixture.
Garnish with parsley and serve with fat-free crackers.

Serves: 4

Nutrition per Serving
Calories	159
Protein	13 grams
Carbohydrate	27 grams
Cholesterol	6 milligrams
Sodium	1458 milligrams
Dietary Fiber	0 grams

Exchanges
1 meat
1 vegetable
1 starch

HOT BEAN DIP

EASY - DO AHEAD

ingredients:
2 16 oz. cans fat-free refried beans
3 cups fat-free Cheddar cheese
1 cup diced tomato
1/2 cup chopped onion
1 4 oz. can chopped green chilies

directions:
Preheat oven to 350 degrees.

Lightly spray a 1 1/2-quart casserole with cooking spray.

Combine refried beans, 2 cups cheese, tomato, onion and chilies and mix well.

Spread bean mixture in casserole and sprinkle remaining 1 cup of cheese on top.

Bake in preheated oven 25 to 30 minutes, until bubbly and cheese is melted.

Serve with fat-free tortilla chips.

Serves: 4

Nutrition per Serving

Calories	395
Protein	38 grams
Carbohydrate	52 grams
Cholesterol	0 milligrams
Sodium	1917 milligrams
Dietary Fiber	7 grams

Exchanges
2 starch
4 vegetable
4 meat

BLACK BEAN DIP
EASY - DO AHEAD

ingredients: 2 cups cooked and drained black beans (or use canned beans)
4 tsp. tomato sauce
3 tbsp. water
1 clove garlic, minced
2 tsp. lemon juice
2 green onions, chopped fine

directions: Place beans, tomato sauce, water, garlic, and lemon juice in a food processor or blender until the mixture forms a smooth paste, about 1 minute.
Put in serving bowl and add chopped onions.
Serve with fat-free crackers.

Serves: 4

Nutrition per Serving

Calories	117
Protein	8 grams
Carbohydrate	21 grams
Cholesterol	0 milligrams
Sodium	31 milligrams
Dietary Fiber	4 grams

Exchanges
1 1/2 starch

VEGETABLE DIP

EASY - DO AHEAD

ingredients:
1/2 tsp. salt
8 1/2 oz. fat-free sour cream
1 1/2 cups fat-free mayonnaise
1 10 oz. package frozen chopped spinach,
drained
2 chopped scallions
1 package Knorr Vegetable Soup Mix
fresh cut-up vegetables

directions:
Mix sour cream and mayonnaise until smooth.
Add remaining ingredients and refrigerate for at
least 4 hours.
Serve with a variety of cut-up vegetables.

Serves: 4

Nutrition per Serving

Calories	140
Protein	6 grams
Carbohydrate	29 grams
Cholesterol	0 milligrams
Sodium	1671 milligrams
Dietary Fiber	2 grams

Exchanges
1 1/2 starch
1 vegetable

MEXICAN LAYER DIP

EASY - DO AHEAD

ingredients:
1 large can fat-free refried beans
1 cup fat-free sour cream
1/2 cup fat-free mayonnaise
1 package taco seasoning
2 cups green onions, chopped
2 4 oz. cans chopped green chilies
2 cups chopped fresh tomatoes
8 to 10 oz. fat-free Cheddar cheese, shredded
Fat-free tortilla chips, crackers, or toasted pita chips

directions:
Spread the beans dip on a large platter.
Mix the sour cream, mayonnaise, and taco seasoning together and spread over the bean dip.
Layer the green onions on the sour cream, then the chilies and tomatoes.
Spread the Cheddar cheese over the top to cover.
Refrigerate and serve at room temperature with fat-free tortilla chips, crackers, or toasted pita chips. This dip is also great with large-sliced vegetables or stuffed in celery.

Serves 10 to 12

Nutrition per Serving		Exchanges
Calories	113	1/2 starch
Protein	12 grams	1/2 meat
Carbohydrate	16 grams	1 vegetable
Cholesterol	0 milligrams	
Sodium	486 milligrams	
Dietary Fiber	1 gram	

NACHO CHEESE DIP

EASY - DO AHEAD

---

ingredients: 8 oz. nonfat cream cheese
1 cup nonfat Mexican shredded cheese
2 tsp. skim milk
1/2 cup medium chunky salsa

directions: In a small saucepan over low heat, combine cream cheese and Cheddar cheese.
Cook until cheese is melted.
Add milk and salsa and continue cooking 10 minutes, until thoroughly heated.
Serve with fat-free chips.

Nutrition per Serving

Calories	50
Protein	8 grams
Carbohydrate	4 grams
Cholesterol	0 milligrams
Sodium	373 milligrams
Dietary Fiber	0 grams

Exchanges

1/3 milk
1/2 meat

HOT AND SPICY TOMATO SALSA

EASY - DO AHEAD - FREEZE

ingredients: 3 tomatoes, chopped
1 15 oz. can tomato puree
6 medium garlic cloves, minced or 2 to 3 tsp. garlic puree
1 4 oz. can diced jalapeño chilies
3 tbsp. onion, chopped
1/3 c. unsweetened apple juice
1/4 c. lemon juice
1/2 to 1 tsp. cayenne pepper
1/2 tsp. pepper
1/4 c. chopped fresh cilantro

directions: In a medium saucepan, combine all ingredients except cilantro.
Bring to a boil over high heat.
Reduce heat to medium; cook, uncovered, 15 minutes, stirring occasionally. Stir in cilantro.
Serve with fat-free tortilla chips.
Salsa can be frozen up to 2 months.

Serves: 16

Nutrition per Serving		Exchanges
Calories	24	1 vegetable
Protein	1 gram	
Carbohydrate	5 grams	
Cholesterol	0 milligrams	
Sodium	224 milligrams	
Dietary Fiber	1 gram	

QUESADILLAS WITH VEGETABLE FILLINGS

EASY - DO AHEAD

ingredients:	1 1/2 cups chopped cooked broccoli 1 cup fat-free shredded Cheddar cheese 1 4 oz. can chopped green chilies, drained 1/3 cup finely chopped green onion 2 tbsp. finely chopped cilantro 12 fat-free corn tortillas
directions:	Combine broccoli, Cheddar cheese, green onion, chilies, and cilantro in a small bowl. Cover and refrigerate until ready to use. Preheat broiler and lightly spray baking sheet with cooking spray. Arrange 1/2 cup vegetable filling along one side of the tortilla. Fold over other side to enclose the filling and form a turnover. Broil quesadillas 1 1/2 to 2 1/2 minutes on each side. Cut into wedges.

Serves: 12

Nutrition per Serving

Calories	130
Protein	7 grams
Carbohydrate	26 grams
Cholesterol	0 milligrams
Sodium	475 milligrams
Dietary Fiber	2 grams

Exchanges

1 starch
1/2 meat
1 vegetable

CREAMY SALSA
EASY - DO AHEAD

---

ingredients: 4 oz. fat-free cream cheese
1/3 cup mild, thick and chunky salsa, drained
pepper to taste

directions: Beat cream cheese in a small bowl until creamy
and smooth.
Mix in salsa and pepper until well combined, and
spread over warm fat-free toast.

Serves: 4

Nutrition per Serving

Calories	35
Protein	4 grams
Carbohydrate	2 grams
Cholesterol	4 milligrams
Sodium	153 milligrams
Dietary Fiber	< 1 gram

Exchanges
1/4 starch
1/2 vegetable

ONION SPREAD

EASY - DO AHEAD

ingredients: 1/2 cup fat-free mayonnaise
8 oz. fat-free cream cheese
1/2 cup chopped green onion
1 tsp. Worcestershire sauce
1/4 tsp. garlic
fat-free crackers

directions: Combine mayonnaise and cream cheese until well blended.
Add remaining ingredients and mix.
Serve with fat-free crackers.

Serves: 4

Nutrition per Serving
Calories	81
Protein	9 grams
Carbohydrate	11 grams
Cholesterol	9 milligrams
Sodium	671 milligrams
Dietary Fiber	< 1 gram

Exchanges
3/4 starch
1/2 meat

HERB AND SHRIMP SPREAD
EASY - DO AHEAD

ingredients: 8 oz. fat-free cream cheese
1/4 cup skim milk
1 tbsp. instant minced onion
1 tsp. Worcestershire sauce
1/2 tsp. seasoned salt
1/2 tsp. marjoram leaves
1/2 tsp. tarragon leaves
2 4 1/2 oz. cans small or medium shrimp,
drained and rinsed
fat-free crackers or fresh cut-up vegetables

directions: Mix cream cheese and milk until smooth.
Add onion, Worcestershire sauce, seasoned salt,
marjoram and tarragon, mixing well.
Fold in shrimp.
Cover and chill at least 2 hours.
Serve with fat-free crackers or vegetables.

Serves: 6

Nutrition per Serving		Exchanges
Calories	98	2 meat
Protein	17 grams	1/2 milk
Carbohydrate	5 grams	
Cholesterol	64 milligrams	
Sodium	531 milligrams	
Dietary Fiber	< 1 gram	

ARTICHOKE HEART SPREAD

EASY - DO AHEAD

ingredients: 1 8 oz. can artichoke hearts, drained & finely
chopped
1 c. fat-free Parmesan cheese, grated
1/2 c. fat-free sour cream
1/2 c. fat-free mayonnaise
8 oz. fat-free cream cheese
1/4 tsp. minced garlic
2 jalapeño peppers, diced and seeded (optional)

directions: Preheat oven to 325 degrees.
Mix all ingredients until smooth.
Put mixture in an oven-proof dish and bake for
30 to 45 minutes or until lightly browned.
Serve with fat-free crackers or sourdough bread.

Serves: 4

Nutrition per Serving

Calories	126
Protein	12 grams
Carbohydrate	17 grams
Cholesterol	0 milligrams
Sodium	565 milligrams
Dietary Fiber	0 grams

Exchanges
1 meat
3/4 starch
1 vegetable

ELEGANT COLD VEGGIE PLATTER

EASY - DO AHEAD

ingredients:
1 16 oz. can baby beets
1 lb. cauliflower flowerets, cooked and chilled
1 lb. baby carrots, cooked and chilled
1 lb. fresh string beans, cooked and chilled
1 lb. asparagus, cooked and chilled
1 cup fat-free mayonnaise
1/2 c. fat-free sour cream
2 tbsp. lemon juice
1 tsp. seasoned salt-substitute
1/2 cup frozen chopped spinach, thawed and drained well

directions:
Blend mayonnaise, sour cream, lemon juice, salt substitute, and spinach until mixture is smooth. Refrigerate several hours before serving.
Arrange cooked vegetables around serving dish and place cold dip in the center.

Serves: 12

Nutrition per Serving
Calories	77
Protein	3 grams
Carbohydrate	16 grams
Cholesterol	0 milligrams
Sodium	260 milligrams
Dietary Fiber	< 1 gram

Exchanges
2 1/2 vegetable
1/4 starch

DR. RICK'S CRAB APPETIZER RECIPE

EASY - DO AHEAD

ingredients:
12 oz. fat-free Philadelphia cream cheese
12 oz. Crosse & Blackwell seafood cocktail sauce
8 oz. fat-free imitation crabmeat
fat-free crackers

directions:
Soften cream cheese and spread on platter.
Pour cocktail sauce over the cream cheese.
Break up the crabmeat into small pieces and spread over the cocktail sauce.
Serve with fat-free crackers.
Best served at room temperature. Do not put crackers around dip, because they will get soggy.

Serves: 6

Nutrition per Serving

Calories	164
Protein	12 grams
Carbohydrate	25 grams
Cholesterol	14 milligrams
Sodium	1480 milligrams
Dietary Fiber	No Data

Exchanges

1 meat
1 1/2 starch

Dr. Rick Shaikewitz, Chiropractic Physician,
Chandler, Arizona

"UNFRIED" FRIED ZUCCHINI AND MUSHROOMS

EASY - DO AHEAD

ingredients:
2 large zucchini
16 fresh mushrooms
1/2 to 1 cup fat-free egg substitute
1 to 1 1/2 cups cornflake crumbs
garlic and onion powder to taste

directions:
Wash zucchini and slice into 1/2 to 3/4-inch thick round pieces.

Preheat oven to 400 degrees.

Dip zucchini and mushrooms into egg substitute and then coat with cornflake crumbs seasoned with garlic and onion powder.

Place coated vegetables on cookie sheet lined with foil and bake 15 to 20 minutes, or until the outside is crispy and vegetables are cooked through.

Great served with fat-free honey mustard or ranch dressing.

Serves: 8

Nutrition per Serving

Calories	83	
Protein	4 grams	
Carbohydrate	17 grams	
Cholesterol	0 milligrams	
Sodium	214 milligrams	
Dietary Fiber	< 1 gram	

Exchanges
2 vegetable
1/2 starch

HONEY-CHEESE CREPES

AVERAGE - DO AHEAD - FREEZE

ingredients:
1/2 cup flour
2/3 cup skim milk
1 large egg white
1/2 cup nonfat cottage cheese
2 tsp. honey
1/8 tsp. ginger
cinnamon to taste

directions:
Combine the milk and egg white in a small bowl.
Add the milk mixture to the flour, stirring just to combine the ingredients.
Lightly spray a nonstick skillet with cooking spray and set over moderately high heat.
When the skillet is hot, pour in 2 tablespoons of the batter, turning the pan to make a thin pancake.
Cook for 30 seconds on each side, or until the crepe is golden brown.
Transfer to a plate, top with wax paper, and repeat until all the batter is used.
Combine the cottage cheese, honey, ginger, and cinnamon, and blend until mixture is very smooth.
Spread each crepe with a tablespoon of cheese mixture, fold in half, then fold in half again.
The crepes can be prepared in advance, stacked between sheets of wax paper, wrapped, and frozen.
Thaw before serving.

Serves: 4

Nutrition per Serving

Calories	105
Protein	7 grams
Carbohydrate	17 grams
Cholesterol	3 milligrams
Sodium	126 milligrams
Dietary Fiber	< 1 gram

Exchanges
1/2 meat
1 starch

ONION CHEESE PUFFS

EASY - DO AHEAD

---

ingredients:
1 cup fat-free mayonnaise
1 cup fat-free Parmesan cheese
1/2 cup onion, grated, or 1 tbsp. onion powder
3/4 tbsp. skim milk
fat-free crackers, assorted

directions:
Combine the mayonnaise, cheese, onion, and milk, and mix well.
Spread the mixture on crackers and place under broiler for 2 minutes, or in a 350° oven until brown.

Serves: 6

Nutrition per Serving
(crackers not included)

Calories	72
Protein	5 grams
Carbohydrate	12 grams
Cholesterol	0 milligrams
Sodium	401 milligrams
Dietary Fiber	< 1 gram

Exchanges

1/2 milk
1 vegetable

STUFFED MUSHROOMS

EASY - DO AHEAD

ingredients: 10 medium mushrooms, cleaned
1/2 cup fat-free cottage cheese
1/2 tsp. beef bouillon granules
1/2 tsp. dried chives
1/4 tsp. Worcestershire sauce

directions: Remove stems from mushrooms and set caps aside. Mix cottage cheese, bouillon granules, chives, and Worcestershire sauce in a blender or food processor until smooth.
Stuff each mushroom cap with cheese mixture and refrigerate until ready to serve.

Serves: 4

Nutrition per Serving

Calories	28
Protein	4 grams
Carbohydrate	2 grams
Cholesterol	2 milligrams
Sodium	96 milligrams
Dietary Fiber	0 grams

Exchanges
1 vegetable

ARTICHOKE PITA CHIPS

AVERAGE

ingredients:
1/4 cup water
1 9 oz. package frozen artichoke hearts
1 cup thinly-sliced celery
2 green onions, sliced
1 cup nonfat cottage cheese
1/3 cup fat-free mayonnaise
1 tbsp. lemon juice
8 small pita pockets
grated fat-free Parmesan cheese (optional)

directions:
Preheat oven to 400°.
Combine artichokes, water, and celery in a small saucepan, and simmer, covered, for 15 minutes. Drain well.
Combine artichoke mixture and onions and chop finely in a food processor.
Scrape this into a large bowl.
Puree the cottage cheese in the processor and add the pureed cottage cheese, mayonnaise, and lemon juice to the artichoke mixture.
Split pitas in half and spread with 3 tablespoons artichoke mixture (on rough side of pita), sprinkle on cheese (if desired), and cut into 4 wedges.
Arrange on baking sheets and bake in a preheated oven for 10 to 15 minutes or until heated through and the edges are brown.
Serve immediately.

Serves: 5 dozen

Nutrition per Serving
Calories:	157
Protein	11 grams
Cholesterol	4 milligrams
Carbohydrate	27 grams
Sodium	500 milligrams
Dietary Fiber	< 1 gram

Exchanges
1 meat
1 starch
2 vegetable

CRAB DEVILS

EASY

---

ingredients: 1 package fat-free crabmeat, drained, or imitation fat-free crab flakes
3/4 cup fat-free mayonnaise
1/2 cup fat-free Parmesan cheese
1/2 tsp. Worcestershire sauce
Tabasco to taste
onion powder to taste
pimento strips and parsley for garnish
fat-free onion crackers

directions: Combine crabmeat, mayonnaise, cheese,
Worcestershire sauce, Tabasco, and onion powder
and mix well.
Spread on onion crackers or crisps.
Sprinkle with extra Parmesan cheese and broil
until lightly browned and bubbly.
Cool slightly, and garnish with pimento and pars-
ley, if desired.

Serves: 6

Nutrition per Serving

Calories	72
Protein	9 grams
Carbohydrate	7 grams
Cholesterol	18 milligrams
Sodium	629 milligrams
Dietary Fiber	0 grams

Exchanges
1 meat
1/2 starch

SENSATIONAL SOUPS & SANDWICHES

TUNA CHOWDER

EASY - DO AHEAD

ingredients:
8 mushrooms, sliced
2 stalks celery, diced
1 medium onion, diced
1 large potato, diced
4 cups fat-free chicken broth
12 oz. evaporated skim milk
4 6 oz. cans of StarKist chunk light tuna in spring water (do not drain)
salt and pepper, to taste
cornstarch, optional

directions:
Combine mushrooms, celery, onion, potato and broth in a large pot.
Add evaporated skim milk and chunk light tuna. Bring to a boil, reduce heat, cover and simmer for 30 minutes, stirring occasionally.
Add 1 to 2 tablespoons cornstarch if thicker soup is desired.

Serves: 8

Nutrition per Serving

Calories	183
Protein	30 grams
Carbohydrate	13 grams
Cholesterol	17 milligrams
Sodium	818 milligrams
Dietary Fiber	1 gram

Exchanges
3 meat
1 milk

CREAM OF VEGETABLE SOUP

EASY - DO AHEAD

ingredients: 2 cups fat-free chicken broth
2 10 oz. packages frozen vegetables (spinach, broccoli, carrot, zucchini, etc., or combination)
1 cup cooked rice
2 cups skim milk
pepper to taste
1/2 tsp. onion powder
1/2 tsp. garlic powder

directions: Place chicken broth and vegetables in a large saucepan over high heat and bring to a boil.
Reduce heat to low, cover, and simmer until vegetables are tender.
Stir vegetables several times during cooking.
Pour half of the broth, half the vegetables, and
cooked rice into a blender and blend at low speed
until smooth.
Pour soup mixture into a large bowl and repeat
blending with the remaining chicken broth and
vegetables.
Stir skim milk into soup and refrigerate until chilled.
The soup may be served hot or cold.

Serves: 6

Nutrition per Serving		**Exchanges**
Calories	98	1/2 milk
Protein	6 grams	2 vegetable
Carbohydrate	18 grams	
Cholesterol	1 milligram	
Sodium	387 milligrams	
Dietary Fiber	1 gram	

BLACK-BEAN CHILI

EASY - DO AHEAD

ingredients:
1 large onion, chopped
2 red bell peppers, seeded and chopped
1 tbsp. chopped jalapeño pepper
10 mushrooms, quartered
6 small tomatoes, cut in large chunks
1 cup frozen corn kernels, thawed and drained
1 tsp. pepper
1 tsp. ground cumin
1 tbsp. chili powder
4 cups canned black beans, rinsed
1 1/2 cups fat-free chicken broth
1 10 oz. package frozen chopped spinach,
thawed and drained

directions:
Lightly spray a nonstick skillet with cooking spray.
Add onion, red pepper, jalapeño pepper, mushrooms, tomatoes, corn, pepper, cumin and chili powder.
Cook over medium-high heat for 10 minutes.
Add beans and chicken broth and boil for 10 minutes.
Remove 1 1/2 cups bean mixture from skillet and place in blender or food processor. Blend mixture until pureed. Return to saucepan and add spinach.
Cook 5 to 6 minutes until spinach is well heated.

Serves: 6

Nutrition per Serving
Calories   95
Protein   6 grams
Carbohydrate   15 grams
Cholesterol   0 milligrams
Sodium   486 milligrams
Dietary Fiber   4 grams

Exchanges
1/2 starch
2 vegetable

VEGETABLE SOUP

AVERAGE - DO AHEAD

ingredients: 3 1/4 cups fat-free chicken broth, divided
1 1/4 lb. yams, peeled and cut into 1/2" chunks
3 carrots, peeled and cut into 1/2" chunks
1 1/2 cups diced onions
8 oz. mushrooms, sliced
2 garlic cloves, peeled and halved
1 tsp. Italian seasoning
1/2 tsp. pepper
5 cups water
3/4 cup small pasta
1 10 oz. package frozen peas
1 10 oz. package frozen leaf spinach

directions: Heat 2 to 3 tablespoons chicken broth in a large soup pot over medium-high heat until hot.
Add yams, carrots, onions, mushrooms, garlic, Italian seasoning and pepper.
Cook the vegetables, stirring, until the vegetables begin to brown.
Add the chicken broth and water to the pot and bring to a boil.
Reduce the heat to low, cover and simmer 20 minutes.
Bring the soup to a boil again, over medium-high heat, and stir in the pasta. Cook uncovered 5 minutes.
Stir in the peas and spinach and return soup to a boil. Continue cooking until the pasta is tender, about 5 minutes.

Serves: 8

Nutrition per Serving		Exchanges
Calories	251	2 starch
Protein	7 grams	4 vegetable
Carbohydrate	56 grams	
Cholesterol	0 milligrams	
Sodium	444 milligrams	
Dietary Fiber	3 grams	

BEAN AND CABBAGE SOUP

EASY - DO AHEAD

ingredients:
4 cups fat-free beef broth
1 cup water
8 cups (1 medium) coarsely chopped cabbage
1 1/2 cups sliced carrots
1 cup sliced onion
1/2 tsp. ground allspice
1 19 oz. can white kidney beans,
rinsed and drained
2 tbsp. dried dill
fat-free sour cream (optional)

directions:
Bring broth, water, cabbage, carrots, onion and allspice to a boil in a large soup pot.
Reduce heat, cover, and simmer 15 minutes until vegetables are crisp-tender.
Add beans and dill and simmer, uncovered, 5 minutes.
Garnish with sour cream, if desired.

Serves: 6

Nutrition per Serving

Calories	213
Protein	11 grams
Carbohydrate	42 grams
Cholesterol	3 milligrams
Sodium	1392 milligrams
Dietary Fiber	13 grams

Exchanges
1 1/2 starch
4 vegetable

CHILLED STRAWBERRY SOUP

AVERAGE - DO AHEAD

ingredients:
3 pints strawberries
1/2 cup red wine
1/2 cup orange juice
1/3 cup honey
3 cups water
1/2 cup fat-free sour cream (optional)

directions:
Clean strawberries and remove stems.
If the strawberries are very large, cut them in half, and set aside.
In a deep saucepan, over medium-low heat, combine the red wine, orange juice and honey with water and bring the liquid to a simmer.
Remove the pan from heat and add the strawberries.
Allow soup to cool.
In a blender, puree the strawberries and liquid in several batches until the mixture is smooth.
Transfer to another bowl and chill.
Fat-free sour cream may be added just before serving, if desired.

Serves: 4

Nutrition per Serving
Calories	155
Protein	1 gram
Carbohydrate	34 grams
Cholesterol	0 milligrams
Sodium	4 milligrams
Dietary Fiber	3 grams

Exchanges
2 1/2 fruit

MINESTRONE SOUP

AVERAGE - DO AHEAD - FREEZE

ingredients:
2 15 oz. cans kidney beans
2 cloves garlic, minced
1/4 tsp. pepper
1/4 cup chopped fresh parsley
1 unpeeled zucchini, diced
2 stalks celery, chopped
1 carrot, diced
2 green onions, chopped
1 10 oz. package frozen chopped spinach, thawed and drained well
1 8 oz. can tomato sauce or 1 lb. canned tomatoes
2 1/2 cups water
1/2 dry sherry
1/4 cup macaroni, rotini, shells, or other pasta

directions:
Place kidney beans in a large soup pot and mash until 2/3 of the beans are broken
Add garlic, pepper, parsley, and stir.
Add the remaining vegetables, tomatoes and water.
Simmer 1 hour over low heat.
Add sherry and cook 10 minutes.
Add macaroni or other pasta and cook over high heat 15 minutes.
Sprinkle with fat-free Parmesan cheese for added flavor and garnish.
Any low-salt ingredients can be substituted for the beans and tomatoes.

Serves: 6

Nutrition per Serving

Calories	220
Protein	13 grams
Carbohydrate	40 grams
Cholesterol	0 milligrams
Sodium	855 milligrams
Dietary Fiber	11 grams

Exchanges
2 starch
2 vegetable

FAT-FREE MATZO BALLS
EASY - DO AHEAD - FREEZE

ingredients:
4 egg whites
1/2 cup matzo meal
2 tsp. dried onions
1/2 tsp. cinnamon
1 tsp. dried parsley
1/4 tsp. pepper

directions:
Beat egg whites in a large bowl until stiff.
Fold in mixture of matzo meal and seasonings.
Let stand 15 minutes.
Form mixture into small balls. (You can spray the palms of your hands with cooking spray and water in order to keep balls from sticking.)
Drop matzo balls into boiling water or soup.
Cover pot and simmer for 30 minutes.
Matzo balls freeze well and can be added to soup when ready for serving.

Makes: 10 medium-size matzo balls

Nutrition per Serving		**Exchanges**
Calories	36	1/2 starch
Protein	2 grams	
Carbohydrate	7 grams	
Cholesterol	0 milligrams	
Sodium	22 milligrams	
Dietary Fiber	0 grams	

CHICKEN-FLAVORED VEGETABLE SOUP

EASY - DO AHEAD - FREEZE

ingredients: 8 cans fat-free chicken broth
6 carrots, peeled and chunked
6 to 8 stalks of celery, cut in large pieces
fresh broccoli florets or 16 oz. frozen cut broccoli
fresh cauliflower florets or 16 oz. frozen cauliflower
fresh or frozen green beans (16 oz.)

directions: Bring chicken broth to a boil in a large soup pot.
Add carrots and celery and cook over medium
heat for 20 minutes, or until tender.
Add broccoli, cauliflower and green beans and
continue cooking 20 to 30 minutes. If using frozen
vegetables, cook in hot soup according to package
directions.
Fat-free noodles or matzo balls can be added.
If using noodles, bring the soup to a boil and add
noodles for the last ten minutes of cooking.

Serves: 8

Nutrition per Serving

Calories	115
Protein	13 grams
Carbohydrate	18 grams
Cholesterol	0 milligrams
Sodium	654 milligrams
Dietary Fiber	7 grams

Exchanges
4 vegetable

GAZPACHO SOUP

EASY - DO AHEAD

ingredients: 3 large cans Mexican-style stewed tomatoes
3 stalks celery
1 green pepper
1 red pepper
1 4 oz. can chopped green chilies
1 to 2 cucumbers
2 tbsp. Worcestershire sauce
1 tsp. garlic powder
1 tsp. onion powder
Pepper to taste

directions: Pour the stewed tomatoes, with juice, into a large bowl.
Chop all vegetables into chunky pieces and add chopped green chilies.
Combine all other ingredients and chill before serving.
This soup keeps well in refrigerator for several days.

Serves: 8

Nutrition per Serving

Calories	94
Protein	3 grams
Carbohydrate	23 grams
Cholesterol	0 milligrams
Sodium	880 milligrams
Dietary Fiber	3 grams

Exchanges
4 vegetable

FRENCH ONION SOUP

AVERAGE - DO AHEAD - FREEZE

ingredients:
5 lb. fresh yellow or Vidalia onions, sliced thin
6 to 8 oz. Promise Ultra fat-free margarine
10 10 1/2 oz. cans of beef broth
3/4 cup flour
paprika
pepper to taste
fat-free sourdough or French bread
fat-free Swiss or mozzarella cheese

directions:
Melt the fat-free margarine in a large soup pot. Add the sliced onions to the melted margarine and simmer on low heat for two hours. Drain the liquid from the cooked onions, but leave enough liquid to thoroughly coat the onions.

Add the flour, paprika and pepper to the soup and cook for about 10 minutes, until the onion mixture becomes thickened.

Add the beef broth, cover, and cook on low heat for 1 1/2 hours. Slice the bread and bake in the oven at 350 degrees for about ten minutes on each side, until the bread is toasty and cooked through.

Place one piece of bread in each soup bowl and cover with soup. Top with cheese.

Place under heated broiler and cook until cheese is melted.

This soup is best if made a day ahead, refrigerated, and heated before serving.

Serves: 12 large bowls

Nutrition per Serving		Exchanges
Calories	149	1/2 starch
Protein	17 grams	3 vegetable
Carbohydrate	20 grams (without bread)	1 meat
Cholesterol	8 milligrams	
Sodium	1749 milligrams	
Dietary Fiber	3 grams	

BLACK BEAN SOUP

AVERAGE - DO AHEAD - FREEZE

ingredients:

1 2/3 cups fat-free chicken broth, divided
1 large onion, chopped
2 cloves garlic, minced
1/2 tsp. dried oregano, crushed
1/4 tsp. dried thyme, crushed
1/4 tsp. ground cumin
cayenne pepper to taste
1 1/2 cups black beans, cooked and drained

directions:

In a large saucepan over moderate heat, heat 2 to 4 teaspoons chicken broth until hot.

Add the onion and garlic and cook, uncovered, until the onion is soft.

Stir in the oregano, thyme, cumin, and cayenne pepper, and cook for 1 minute, stirring continuously. Place half the cooked beans in a blender or food processor and puree for 30 seconds.

Add the bean puree, the remaining beans, and the remaining chicken broth to the saucepan, reduce the heat to low, and cook, uncovered, for 15 minutes.

Serves: 4

Nutrition per Serving

Calories	107
Protein	6 grams
Carbohydrate	20 grams
Cholesterol	0 milligrams
Sodium	376 milligrams
Dietary Fiber	3 grams

Exchanges

1 1/4 starch

MUSHROOM-BARLEY SOUP

EASY - DO AHEAD - FREEZE

ingredients:	2 yellow onions, chopped
	3 carrots, peeled and sliced
	1/2 pound mushrooms, sliced
	4 cups fat-free beef broth
	1/4 cup chopped parsley
	1/2 cup barley
	pepper to taste
directions:	Place all the ingredients in a large pot and bring to a boil over moderately high heat.
	Lower heat so the mixture boils gently, and simmer, partly covered, for 40 minutes or until the barley is tender.

Serves: 4

Nutrition per Serving

Calories	166
Protein	5 grams
Carbohydrate	36 grams
Cholesterol	0 milligrams
Sodium	926 milligrams
Dietary Fiber	7 grams

Exchanges
2 vegetable
1 1/2 starch

VEGGIE PITA POCKET SANDWICHES

EASY

---

ingredients:

4 6-inch pita pockets
1 cup broccoli florets, chopped
1 cup thinly sliced carrots
1 cup thinly sliced mushrooms
3 green onions, thinly sliced
4 tbsp. fat-free ranch salad dressing
1 cup alfalfa sprouts

directions:

Combine broccoli, carrots, mushrooms, and green onions in a microwave-safe baking dish, cover with vented plastic wrap, and cook 6 to 8 minutes, or until all the vegetables are tender.

Cover pita pockets with paper towels and cook on HIGH 1 minute, or until well heated.

Cut a slice from the top of each pita pocket and fill with the warm vegetable mixture.

Top with alfalfa sprouts and ranch dressing.

Serves: 4

Nutrition per Serving		Exchanges
Calories	141	1 starch
Protein:	6 grams	2 vegetable
Carbohydrate	28 grams	
Cholesterol	0 milligrams	
Sodium	292 milligrams	
Dietary Fiber	3 grams	

MUSHROOM-CHEESE SANDWICH

EASY

ingredients: 1/3 cup fat-free chicken broth
3 tbsp. white wine
2 cups sliced fresh mushrooms
1 red bell pepper, sliced
1 cup sliced scallions (whites only)
2 cups fat-free grated mozzarella cheese
8 slices fat-free sourdough bread (or bread of choice)
spicy mustard

directions: Heat the chicken broth and wine in a nonstick skillet.
Add mushrooms, red pepper, and scallions and cook until the liquid is evaporated.
Toast the bread lightly.
Spread each bread slice with mustard and top with mushroom mixture.
Sprinkle grated mozzarella cheese over top of mushroom mixture and broil until cheese is melted.
Serve sandwich open-faced.

Serves: 8

Nutrition per Serving

Calories	150
Protein	20 grams
Carbohydrate	13 grams
Cholesterol	1 milligrams
Sodium	619 milligrams
Dietary Fiber	2.6 grams

Exchanges
2 vegetables
3 meat

SUPER SEAFOOD SALAD SANDWICH

EASY - DO AHEAD

ingredients: 2 cups fat-free Crab or Lobster Delights, flake-style
1/2 cup fat-free mayonnaise
2 stalks celery, chopped
3 tbsp. finely chopped onion
fat-free bread, bialy, or pita pocket

directions: Cut crab or lobster flakes in half or shred.
Combine with mayonnaise, celery and onion.
Serve as a sandwich on fat-free bread, bialy, or a
pita pocket.

Serves: 2

Nutrition per Serving		Exchanges
Calories	137	1 meat
Protein	9 grams	1 1/4 starch
Carbohydrate	24 grams	
Cholesterol	10 milligrams	
Sodium	951 milligrams	
Dietary Fiber	1 gram	

* Nutritional analysis without bread.

EGG SALAD SANDWICHES

EASY - DO AHEAD

ingredients:
1 1/2 cups fat-free egg substitute
1/3 cup fat-free mayonnaise
1 1/2 tsp. fat-free Dijon mustard
1/2 cup frozen tiny green peas, thawed
1/3 cup chopped bell pepper
1/3 cup chopped celery
1/4 cup finely chopped red onion
1/4 tsp. pepper
fat-free bread, bialy, or pita pocket

directions:
Lightly spray a nonstick skillet with cooking spray and heat over low heat.

Add egg substitute and cook, without stirring, 18 minutes or until set and no wet spots remain.

Mix mayonnaise and mustard in a medium-size bowl.

Stir in peas, bell pepper, celery, onion and pepper. Remove egg substitute from stove and chop coarsely or dice. Add to vegetable mixture and stir until blended. Spoon into bread, bialy, or pita pocket.

Serves: 4

Nutrition per Serving

Calories	134
Protein	12 grams
Carbohydrate	19 grams
Cholesterol	0 milligrams
Sodium	430 milligrams
Dietary Fiber	1 gram

Exchanges
1 1/2 starch
1 meat

GRILLED HOAGIE SANDWICHES

EASY - DO AHEAD

ingredients:
1/3 cup fat-free shredded Cheddar cheese
3 tbsp. fat-free mayonnaise
1 tbsp. honey mustard
4 fat-free French bread rolls, bialys, pita pockets, or sliced fat-free bread (8 slices)
8 oz. fat-free sliced turkey breast
4 thin tomato slices, halved
2 thin onion slices, separated into rings
1/2 medium-size green bell pepper, thinly sliced

directions:
Heat oven to 450 degrees.
In a small bowl, combine the cheese, mayonnaise and mustard and mix well.
Spread 1 tablespoon mayonnaise mixture on each cut side of the rolls.
Layer 1/4 each of the turkey, tomato, onion and bell pepper on the bottom half of each roll or bread. Cover with top halves of rolls and wrap sandwich in heavy-duty foil.
Place foil packets on cookie sheet. Bake at 450 degrees for 10 to 15 minutes, or until thoroughly heated and cheese is melted.

Serves: 4

Nutrition per Serving		Exchanges
Calories	190	1 1/2 starch
Protein	15 grams	1 1/2 meat
Carbohydrate	27 grams	
Cholesterol	20 milligrams	
Sodium	1056 milligrams	
Dietary Fiber	1 gram	

PRETZELS
DIFFICULT - DO AHEAD - FREEZE

ingredients:

1 envelope (1/4 oz.) active dry yeast
3/4 cup warm water (105-115 degrees)
2 1/2 cups whole wheat or all-purpose flour
1 large egg white beaten with 1 tsp. water

directions:

Combine yeast and water in a large bowl; let stand about 5 minutes. Stir until yeast dissolves. Stir 1 1/2 cups flour into yeast mixture; beat with a spoon until smooth. Turn dough onto a lightly floured surface; knead for 5 minutes. Lightly spray a large bowl with cooking spray, shape the dough into a ball, place it in the bowl, and turn several times.

Cover the bowl with a clean dish towel and let the dough rise in a warm place until it is doubled in bulk (about 1 1/2 hours).

Punch the dough down, divide it in half, and cut each half into 6 pieces. Roll each piece into an 18-inch stand.

Twist into a pretzel shape, tucking ends under.

Lightly coat baking sheet with cooking spray, place pretzels on it about 1-inch apart, and cover loosely with a towel.

Let the pretzels rise for 30 minutes.

Preheat the oven to 400 degrees.

Brush the pretzels with the egg white and bake for 10 to 15 minutes or until browned.

This recipe can also be used to make bread-sticks. Bake 20 minutes at 350 degrees. Add garlic or onion powder to dough for flavor.

Serves: 12 pretzels or 36 breadsticks

Nutrition per Serving		**Exchanges**
Calories	98	1 1/4 starch
Protein	3 grams	
Carbohydrate	20 grams	
Cholesterol	0 milligrams	
Sodium	5 milligrams	
Dietary Fiber	0 milligrams	

FAT-FREE FRENCH BREAD
EASY - DO AHEAD - FREEZE - BREAD MACHINE

ingredients: 2 1/2 tsp. dry yeast
3 cups bread flour
1/2 tsp. salt
1 1/2 tsp. sugar
1 1/2 cup water

directions: Put all the ingredients in a bread machine and set
for French bread cycle on medium brown crust.

Serves: 8

Nutrition per Serving

Calories	192
Protein	7 grams
Carbohydrate	39 grams
Cholesterol	0 milligrams
Sodium	136 milligrams
Dietary Fiber	2 grams

Exchanges
2 1/2 starch

GARLIC BREAD

EASY - DO AHEAD

ingredients:
1 lb. loaf fat-free French or sourdough bread
1/2 cup fat-free mayonnaise
1/4 cup fat-free Parmesan cheese
1 1/2 to 2 tsp. minced garlic

directions:
Preheat oven to 450 degrees.
Combine the mayonnaise, cheese, and garlic in a small bowl and blend well.
Slice the bread in half lengthwise and spread the cheese mixture on both halves of the bread.
Place bread on cookie sheet or foil and bake in preheated oven for 10 minutes or until well heated.

Serves: 6

Nutrition per Serving

Calories	130
Protein	7 grams
Carbohydrate	4 grams
Cholesterol	0 milligrams
Sodium	437 milligrams
Dietary Fiber	5 grams

Exchanges
1 1/2 starch

BRAVO
BREAKFAST/BRUNCH

BROCCOLI-CAULIFLOWER FRITTATA

EASY- DO AHEAD

ingredients: 1 10 oz. package frozen cauliflower, thawed
1 10 oz. package frozen broccoli, thawed
3/4 cup fat-free egg substitute
1/2 envelope onion soup mix
1/2 cup fat-free mayonnaise
1/2 cup fat-free cracker crumbs

directions: Drain thawed cauliflower and broccoli.
Mash vegetables and mix with beaten egg substitute, onion soup mix and mayonnaise.
Lightly spray a 9x13-inch baking dish and sprinkle with cracker crumbs.
Pour vegetable mixture in baking dish, top with additional cracker crumbs, and bake at 350 degrees for 45 minutes.

Serves: 6

Nutrition per Serving

		Exchanges
Calories	70	1 vegetable
Protein	5 grams	1/2 starch
Carbohydrate	13 grams	
Cholesterol	0 milligrams	
Sodium	610 milligrams	
Dietary Fiber	3 grams	

VEGETABLE FRITTATA

EASY - DO AHEAD

ingredients: 2 10 oz. packages frozen cauliflower, broccoli or spinach
3/4 cup fat-free egg substitute
1/2 envelope dry onion soup mix
1/2 cup fat-free mayonnaise
matzo meal or fat-free bread crumbs

directions: Preheat oven to 350 degrees.
Defrost frozen vegetables, drain, and mash well.
Mix mashed vegetables with egg substitute, onion soup mix, and mayonnaise.
Lightly spray a 9x13-inch baking dish with cooking spray and sprinkle with matzo meal or bread crumbs.
Pour in vegetable-egg mixture and top with additional matzo meal, if desired.
Bake in preheated oven for 45 minutes or until eggs are set.

Serves: 6

Nutrition per Serving

Calories	83
Protein	5 grams
Carbohydrate	13 grams
Cholesterol	0 milligrams
Sodium	785 milligrams
Dietary Fiber	1 gram

Exchanges
1 vegetable
3/4 starch

CONFETTI CORN FRITTATA

EASY

---

ingredients: 1 1/2 cups frozen corn, red-and-green pepper mixture, thawed and drained
2 cartons (8 oz. each) fat-free egg substitute
pepper to taste

directions: Preheat oven to 350 degrees.
Lightly spray nonstick skillet with cooking spray and heat over medium heat.
Pour corn mixture into bowl and stir in egg substitute and pepper.
Pour corn-egg mixture into hot skillet.
As the eggs cook, continue stirring and shaking skillet back and forth, until it is firm on the bottom and almost set on top.
Bake in a preheated 350 degree oven for 3 to 5 minutes.
Great brunch food served with fat-free toast and creamy salsa.

Serves: 4

Nutrition per Serving
Calories   94
Protein   8 grams
Carbohydrate   16 grams
Cholesterol   0 milligrams
Sodium   396 milligrams
Dietary Fiber   2 grams

Exchanges
1/2 meat
1 starch

CRUSTLESS SPINACH QUICHE

EASY - DO AHEAD

ingredients:
16 oz. fat-free egg substitute
1/3 cup flour
1 tsp. baking powder
16 oz. nonfat cottage cheese
1 10 oz. package frozen chopped spinach, thawed and squeezed dry*
1/4 cup thinly sliced green onions
1/4 tsp. cayenne pepper

directions:
Preheat oven to 400 degrees.
Lightly spray a 10-inch quiche or pie dish with cooking spray.
Mix all filling ingredients in a large bowl.
Pour into pie dish and bake 15 minutes.
Lower heat to 350 degrees and bake 35 to 40 minutes longer, until filling is set and a toothpick inserted in the center comes out clean.
Let cool 10 minutes on wire rack before serving.
*Chopped broccoli may be substituted for the spinach.

Serves: 8

Nutrition per Serving

Calories	92
Protein	12 grams
Carbohydrate	9 grams
Cholesterol	1 milligram
Sodium	279 milligrams
Dietary Fiber	1 gram

Exchanges
1 meat
2 vegetable

BREAKFAST BURRITO

EASY

---

ingredients:
2 7-inch fat-free flour tortillas
1 small container fat-free Egg Beaters
1/4 cup fat-free shredded Cheddar cheese
1 small can fat-free refried beans
salsa

directions:
Cook Egg Beaters according to package directions.
Spread beans on tortillas.
Place cooked egg substitute on tortillas and sprinkle with cheese.
Microwave tortillas until cheese is melted.

Serves: 2

<u>**Nutrition per Serving**</u>

		<u>Exchanges</u>
Calories	285	2 starch
Protein	26	3 meat
Carbohydrate	39 grams	1 vegetable
Cholesterol	0 milligrams	
Sodium	929 milligrams	
Dietary Fiber	5 grams	

Suzie Whiting, St. Louis, Missouri

SPINACH-CHEESE BAKE

EASY - DO AHEAD

ingredients:
8 oz. fat-free shredded Cheddar cheese
1 10 oz. package frozen chopped spinach, thawed and well-drained
1 16 oz. container fat-free cottage cheese
3/4 cup fat-free egg substitute
3 tbsp. flour
1/8 tsp. garlic powder
2 oz. fat-free shredded mozzarella cheese
pepper to taste

directions:
Preheat oven to 375 degrees.
Combine all the ingredients except mozzarella cheese in a large bowl, and spoon into a baking dish lightly sprayed with cooking spray.
Top with mozzarella cheese and bake in preheated oven for 45 minutes or until set.
Allow casserole to cool 10 minutes before serving.

Serves: 4

Nutrition per Serving

Calories	148
Protein	23 grams
Carbohydrate	11 grams
Cholesterol	3 milligrams
Sodium	602 milligrams
Dietary Fiber	2 grams

Exchanges

3 meat
2 vegetable

CHILI RELLENO CASSEROLE

EASY - DO AHEAD

---

ingredients:
1 32 oz. can fat-free refried beans
1 tsp. chili powder
2 4 oz. cans diced green chilies
1 lb. fat-free shredded Monterey Jack cheese
1 cup fat-free egg substitute
4 tbsp. flour
1 cup skim milk

directions:
Preheat oven to 350 degrees.
Season the refried beans with chili powder and spread over the bottom of 9x13-inch baking dish, lightly sprayed with cooking spray.
Layer chilies and cheese on top of beans.
Mix the eggs, flour, and milk and blend well.
Spread egg mixture on top of cheese.
Bake in preheated oven 30 to 45 minutes, or until egg mixture is set and slightly brown.

Serves: 8

Nutrition per Serving

Calories	259
Protein	29 grams
Carbohydrate	31 grams
Cholesterol	0 milligrams
Sodium	1168 milligrams
Dietary Fiber	4 grams

Exchanges
2 starch
3 meat

ZUCCHINI, CARROT AND ONION QUICHE

DIFFICULT

ingredients:
1/2 cup long-grain rice
1 cup shredded fat-free Swiss cheese
3 large egg whites
1 onion, sliced thin
1 each carrot and zucchini, grated
1 cup fat-free chicken broth
1/4 cup egg substitute
1 cup skim milk
pepper to taste

directions: Preheat the oven to 350 degrees. Cook the rice according to package directions, omitting any butter or salt. Lightly spray a 9-inch pie pan with cooking spray and set aside. Combine the cooked rice, 2 tablespoons Swiss cheese, and 1 egg white. Lightly moisten hands and press the rice mixture over bottom and sides of pie pan. Bake, uncovered, 5 minutes; remove to cool. Cook onion, carrot, and zucchini in hot chicken broth for 15 minutes over medium heat. Increase heat to high and cook, stirring, until all liquid has evaporated. Transfer vegetable mixture to a bowl to cool for about 20 minutes. Lightly beat the remaining egg whites and egg substitute. Mix the eggs into the vegetable mixture; add milk, pepper, and remaining cheese. Pour mixture into pie dish and bake, uncovered, 20 minutes. Cool 15 minutes before serving.

Serves: 4

Nutrition per Serving		Exchanges
Calories	196	1/2 milk
Protein	13 grams	2 vegetable
Carbohydrate	30 grams	1 1/4 starch
Cholesterol	1 milligram	
Sodium	555 milligrams	
Dietary Fiber	2 grams	

APPLE-CINNAMON-RAISIN BREAD PUDDING

AVERAGE - DO AHEAD

ingredients:
8 slices fat-free multigrain or wheat bread
8 oz. fat-free egg substitute
1/4 cup brown sugar
1/2 tsp. ground cinnamon
2 cups skim milk
1/2 tsp. vanilla
1/2 cup finely chopped apple
1/3 cup golden raisins

directions:
Preheat oven to 350 degrees.
Lightly spray a 2-quart casserole dish with cooking spray.
Beat egg substitute, brown sugar, cinnamon, milk and vanilla in a bowl.
Arrange ingredients, starting with half the bread, 1/2 the chopped apples, 1/2 the raisins, and 1/2 the egg mixture.
Repeat the layers, ending with half the egg mixture.
Set casserole in oven in a large pan filled halfway with boiling water.
Bake at 350 degrees for 1 hour and 15 minutes.

Serves: 4

Nutrition per Serving		Exchanges
Calories	251	2 starch
Protein	15 grams	1 fruit
Carbohydrate	50 grams	1 meat
Cholesterol	2 milligrams	
Sodium	369 milligrams	
Dietary Fiber	5 grams	

APPLE-CINNAMON PUFFY PANCAKE

AVERAGE

---

ingredients:
1 large can apple-cinnamon pie filling
1 1/2 cups raisins (optional)
1/4 cup brown sugar
1/2 tsp. cinnamon
1 cup fat-free egg substitute
1 cup skim milk
1 cup flour
1 tbsp. sugar
powdered sugar (optional)

directions:
Preheat oven to 425 degrees.

Heat apple-cinnamon filling, raisins, brown sugar and cinnamon over medium to low heat until warm, and set aside.

Combine egg substitute, milk, flour, and granulated sugar and mix until smooth.

Lightly spray a nonstick skillet (ovenproof) with cooking spray, and pour in batter.

Spoon raisin-apple mixture evenly over top.

Place skillet in preheated 425 degree oven and bake for 20 minutes or until pancake is puffy and golden brown.

Sprinkle with powdered sugar, if desired.

Cut into wedges to serve.

Serves: 6

Nutrition per Serving

Calories	360
Protein	9 grams
Carbohydrate	74 grams
Cholesterol	0 milligrams
Sodium	138 milligrams
Dietary Fiber	2 grams

Exchanges

1/2 milk
1 starch
4 fruit

BLUEBERRY PANCAKES

EASY - DO AHEAD - FREEZE

---

ingredients:
1 cup plain nonfat yogurt
1 carton Egg Beaters
1/2 tsp. vanilla
1 cup whole wheat flour
1 tbsp. sugar
1 tsp. baking powder
1/2 tsp. baking soda
1 cup frozen blueberries, thawed, washed and drained

directions:
In a large bowl, combine yogurt, Egg Beaters, and vanilla.
In a separate bowl, combine remaining dry ingredients.
Mix dry and liquid ingredients.
Fold in blueberries
Pour 1/4 cup of batter onto a nonstick skillet lightly coated with cooking spray.
When bubbles start to appear, flip the pancake and cook until golden brown.

Serves: 10 large pancakes

Nutrition per Serving		Exchanges
Calories	78	1/2 starch
Protein	5 grams	1/2 fruit
Carbohydrate	14 grams	
Cholesterol	0 milligrams	
Sodium	131 milligrams	
Dietary Fiber	29 milligrams	

OATMEAL PANCAKES

EASY - DO AHEAD

ingredients: 3 tbsp. multigrain oatmeal
3 tbsp. cream of wheat
1 tbsp. brown sugar
1 tsp. vanilla extract
6 egg whites
water
Butter Buds, Equal or syrup

directions: Combine oatmeal, cream of wheat, brown sugar, vanilla, and egg whites in a small bowl.
Mix until all ingredients are well blended.
Add enough water to thin the consistency.
Lightly spray a nonstick skillet and heat over medium-high heat.
Pour mixture into hot skillet and cook until pancake is brown on both sides.
Pancake can be served with Butter Buds and Equal or low-calorie syrup.

Serves: 1

Nutrition per Serving		Exchanges
Calories	283	2 1/2 starch
Protein	25 grams	2 meat
Carbohydrate	42 grams	
Cholesterol	0 milligrams	
Sodium	419 milligrams	
Dietary Fiber	2 grams	

Linda Knapp, Personal Trainer, Fitness Director
Scottsdale, Arizona

ORANGE FRENCH TOAST

EASY - DO AHEAD - FREEZE

ingredients:
1 loaf fat-free sourdough bread, sliced thick
2 cartons fat-free egg substitute, thawed
1/2 cup orange juice
1 tbsp. vanilla extract
2 tbsp. cinnamon
powdered sugar (optional)

directions:
Mix egg substitute, orange juice, vanilla extract and cinnamon in a large bowl.
Place slices of sourdough bread into egg mixture and let soak for 1 minute.
Remove bread slices and place in baking dish.
Pour remaining egg mixture over bread and let it soak for about 15 minutes.
Remove bread slices from egg mixture and sprinkle both sides of the bread with cinnamon.
Lightly spray a nonstick skillet with cooking spray and heat over medium heat.
Cook bread slices over medium heat 5 to 7 minutes, or until both sides of the bread are crisp.
Sprinkle powdered sugar on top (optional) and serve with fresh fruit.
ENJOY!!!

Serves: 8

Nutrition per Serving

Calories	127
Protein	10 grams
Carbohydrate	15 grams
Cholesterol	0 milligrams
Sodium	301 grams
Dietary Fiber	4 grams

Exchanges
1 starch
1 meat

Diane Levy

ORANGE-CHEESE SPREAD SANDWICHES

EASY - DO AHEAD

---

ingredients:
1/2 cup fat-free cream cheese, softened
1 tbsp. honey
1 tsp. grated orange rind
1/2 tsp. vanilla
1/2 cup Grape-Nuts cereal
bialys, wheat bread, or multigrain bread

directions:
Combine cheese, honey, orange rind and vanilla in a small bowl until well blended.
Stir in cereal.
Refrigerate cheese mixture until ready to serve.
Spread 2 tablespoons of the cheese on half the bialy or one slice of bread.
Top with bread or other half of bialy to make sandwich.

Serves: 4

Nutrition per Serving

Calories	173
Protein	10 grams
Carbohydrate	36 grams
Cholesterol	0 milligrams
Sodium	499 milligrams
Dietary Fiber	5 grams

Exchanges
1/2 meat
2 starch

BANANA BERRY SANDWICH

EASY - DO AHEAD

---

ingredients:
1 large ripe banana, cut up
1/4 cup fat-free cottage cheese
1 tbsp. fresh lime juice
6 slices fat-free bread or whole-wheat bialys
banana and strawberry slices for topping

directions:
Combine banana, cheese and lime juice in a food processor or blender, and blend 1 minute or until very smooth.
Refrigerate until ready to use.
Toast the bread or bialys and spread with banana mixture.
Top with overlapping rows of banana and strawberry slices.

Serves: 3

Nutrition per Serving
Calories	120
Protein	6 grams
Carbohydrate	20 grams
Cholesterol	0 milligrams
Sodium	216 milligrams
Dietary Fiber	4 grams

Exchanges
1/2 meat
1/2 starch
1 fruit

STRAWBERRY BANANA BREAD

AVERAGE - DO AHEAD - FREEZE

ingredients:
1 cup chopped strawberries
2 tbsp. plus 1/2 cup sugar
2 cups flour
2 tsp. baking powder
2 medium-size bananas, mashed
1/2 cup skim milk, at room temperature
2 large egg whites, at room temperature, lightly beaten
1 tbsp. applesauce
2 tsp. vanilla

directions:
Preheat oven to 350 degrees.
Lightly coat a loaf pan with cooking spray and dust with flour. In a medium bowl, toss strawberries with 2 tablespoons sugar.
In large bowl, stir together flour, remaining sugar, and baking powder.
In another bowl, stir together bananas, milk, egg whites, applesauce and vanilla.
Make a well in the center of the flour mixture and add milk mixture and stir to combine.
Stir in strawberries.
Empty batter into prepared pan and spread evenly.
Bake for 50 to 60 minutes, or until toothpick inserted in center comes out clean.
Cook on rack 10 minutes before removing from pan.
Store sliced bread in refrigerator.

Serves: 12 slices

Nutrition per Serving		Exchanges
Calories	144	1 starch
Protein	3 grams	1 fruit
Carbohydrate	32 grams	
Cholesterol	0 milligrams	
Sodium	70 milligrams	
Dietary Fiber	1 gram	

CHEESE TOAST
EASY - DO AHEAD

ingredients:
1 cup skim milk
1 tbsp. flour
1 tsp. fat-free Dijon mustard
1/2 tsp. Worcestershire sauce
3 drops Tabasco sauce
1 cup fat-free shredded Cheddar cheese
6 slices fat-free toast, halved

directions:
Combine the milk, flour, mustard, Worcestershire sauce, and Tabasco sauce in a saucepan over moderately low heat until the mixture bubbles gently. Let the mixture simmer for 4 minutes, stirring constantly.

Stir in the cheese, a little at a time, and cook sauce over moderately low heat for 4 minutes or until it is smooth.

(Do not let the mixture boil.)

Divide the toast and spoon the cheese mixture over each portion.

This cheese sauce is great with steamed vegetables.

Serves: 4

Nutrition per Serving
Calories	137
Protein	13 grams
Carbohydrate	20 grams
Cholesterol	1 milligram
Sodium	530 milligrams
Dietary Fiber	3 grams

Exchanges
1 starch
1/2 milk
1/2 meat

CINNAMON BIALY CHIPS
EASY - DO AHEAD

ingredients: 1 dozen bialys
cinnamon
Butter Buds
1/4 cup sugar (optional)

directions: Lightly spray a baking sheet with cooking spray.
Cut each bialy into 3 to 4 thin slices.
Lay bialy slices in a single layer on baking sheet.
Sprinkle Butter Buds over each slice of bialy.
Sprinkle cinnamon over each slice of bialy, and sugar, if desired.
Bake at 350 degrees for 15 to 20 minutes.
Turn oven off and leave in for an extra 5 minutes or until good and crunchy.
Eat warm, or store in plastic bags when cooled.
What a fabulous snack! Fat-free addiction!

Yields: 36 chips (3 chips per serving)

Nutrition per Serving		Exchanges
Calories	99	1 1/4 starch
Protein	3 grams	
Carbohydrate	21 grams	
Cholesterol	0 milligrams	
Sodium	99 milligrams	
Dietary Fiber	3 grams	

Michelle Townsend, St. Louis, Missouri

SWEET CINNAMON-RAISIN SPREAD

EASY - DO AHEAD

ingredients:
1 cup nonfat cottage cheese
2 tbsp. nonfat plain yogurt
1 tbsp. honey
1 tbsp. brown sugar
1/8 tsp. cinnamon
1/2 cup raisins

directions:
Place cottage cheese in a food processor or blender and blend until very smooth, about 1 minute. Combine cheese, yogurt, honey, sugar and cinnamon in a bowl until well blended. Stir in raisins. Refrigerate, covered, at least 2 hours for cheese to set and raisins to soften.
Great with plain or flavored bialys!!

Yields: 1 3/4 cups
Serves: 6

Nutrition per Serving		Exchanges
Calories	65	1/2 fruit
Protein	2 grams	1/2 starch
Carbohydrate	15 grams	
Cholesterol	< 1 milligram	
Sodium	37 milligrams	
Dietary Fiber	< 1 gram	

SUPER
SALADS

CRAB AND VEGETABLE SALAD

AVERAGE - DO AHEAD

ingredients:
1 8 oz. package mushrooms
1 small red onion
2 small red and/or yellow peppers
4 tbsp. chicken broth
2 8 oz. packages imitation crabmeat flakes
1/4 cup white vinegar
1/2 tsp. dried oregano leaves
1 tbsp. Dijon mustard
1/2 tsp. sugar
1/4 tsp. pepper
1 head lettuce

directions:
Slice mushrooms and onion. Cut peppers into thin strips.
In a nonstick skillet over medium heat, in 1 to 2 teaspoons hot chicken broth, cook onion until tender. Add mushrooms, cook until tender, and place vegetable mixture in a large bowl. Add 1 to 2 teaspoons hot chicken broth to skillet as needed, and cook pepper strips until tender-crisp, stirring frequently. Remove from skillet and place in bowl with other vegetables. Gently stir in crabmeat. Mix vinegar, oregano, mustard, sugar, and pepper and pour over crab mixture; toss to coat. Arrange lettuce leaves on platter; spoon crab mixture on top.

Serves: 4

Nutrition per Serving

Calories	168
Protein	11 grams
Carbohydrate	30 grams
Cholesterol	20 milligrams
Sodium	958 milligrams
Dietary Fiber	2 grams

Exchanges
1 meat
1 starch
2 vegetable

PARMESAN-VEGETABLE SALAD

EASY - DO AHEAD

ingredients:
2 cups broccoli florets
2 cups cauliflower florets
1/2 red onion, thinly sliced
1/4 cup grated fat-free Parmesan cheese
1/8 cup sugar
1/4 tsp. dried basil, crushed
1 cup fat-free mayonnaise
1/2 large head lettuce, cut up
1 cup fat-free croutons (Toastettes or home-made)
1 4 oz. can sliced water chestnuts, drained

directions:
Combine broccoli, cauliflower, and onion in a large bowl.
In a small bowl, combine the cheese, sugar, basil, and mayonnaise.
Mix well and add the cheese-mayonnaise mixture to the vegetables.
Toss gently, cover, and refrigerate overnight.
Before serving, add lettuce, croutons, and water chestnuts to vegetables, and toss lightly.

Serves: 8

Nutrition per Serving
Calories	98
Protein	4 grams
Carbohydrate	14 grams
Cholesterol	0 milligrams
Sodium	313 milligrams
Dietary Fiber	1 gram

Exchanges
1/4 starch
3 vegetable

TOMATO SALAD

EASY - DO AHEAD

ingredients: 4 large tomatoes
16 oz. fat-free cottage cheese
fat-free French dressing
lettuce
paprika

directions: Cut out tomato core (leaving tomato intact) and cut into wedges.
Place tomato on lettuce leaf and fill with cottage cheese. Pour a small amount of French dressing over the tomato and sprinkle with paprika.

Serves: 4

Nutrition per Serving

Calories	114
Protein	16 grams
Carbohydrate	11 grams
Cholesterol	10 milligrams
Sodium	414 milligrams
Dietary Fiber	1 gram

Exchanges

2 vegetable
1 1/2 meat

BROCCOLI - CARROT SALAD

EASY - DO AHEAD

ingredients:
1 lb. broccoli florets
2 medium carrots, grated (1 cup)
1/2 cup nonfat plain yogurt
1 scallion (white only), minced
1 tbsp. fat-free Dijon mustard
1 tbsp. fresh lemon juice
1/4 tsp. Worcestershire sauce
1/4 tsp. black pepper

directions:
In a large pot of boiling water, cook broccoli florets until they are bright green and tender-crisp, 3 to 4 minutes.
Drain, rinse under cold water and drain again.
In a large bowl, combine broccoli and carrots. Add yogurt, scallions, mustard, lemon juice, Worcestershire sauce and pepper, and toss until well coated.
Serve salad at room temperature or slightly chilled.

Serves: 6

Nutrition per Serving		Exchanges
Calories	45	2 vegetable
Protein	3 grams	
Carbohydrate	8 grams	
Cholesterol	0 milligrams	
Sodium	77 milligrams	
Dietary Fiber	0 grams	

SWEET AND SOUR SALAD

EASY - DO AHEAD

ingredients:
1/2 cup sugar
1/2 cup water
1 cup white vinegar
2 large cucumbers, sliced thin
2 large carrots, sliced thin
1 cabbage, sliced thin
1 green pepper, chopped (optional)

directions:
Mix sugar, water, and vinegar.
Pour over sliced cucumbers, carrots, cabbage, and green pepper.
Refrigerate one day before serving.
Great with bagels at brunch!!

Serves: 6 to 8

Nutrition per Serving		Exchanges
Calories	97	1 vegetable
Protein	1 gram	1 fruit
Carbohydrate	27 grams	
Cholesterol	0 milligrams	
Sodium	19 milligrams	
Dietary Fiber	2 grams	

MOLDED GAZPACHO SALAD

EASY - DO AHEAD

ingredients:
1 6 ounce package low-calorie lemon gelatin
1 1/2 cups boiling water
1 1/2 cups V8 juice
4 tbsp. fat-free Italian dressing
8 tsp. red wine vinegar
1 cup sliced cauliflower florets
1 cup chopped tomatoes
1 cup chopped celery
1/2 cup chopped green bell pepper

directions:
In a large bowl, dissolve gelatin in boiling water.
Stir in V8 juice, salad dressing, and vinegar.
Chill until partially set.
Fold in cauliflower, tomato, celery, and green pepper.
If desired, pour into a 6-cup mold sprayed lightly with cooking spray, or put in a shallow glass dish.
Chill several hours until firm.

Serves: 8

Nutrition per Serving

Calories	32
Protein	2 grams
Carbohydrate	6 grams
Cholesterol	0 milligrams
Sodium	272 milligrams
Dietary Fiber	1 gram

Exchanges
1 vegetable

HOT SPINACH SALAD

EASY - DO AHEAD

ingredients:
8 cups fresh spinach, cut up
1 small red onion, sliced thin
1 8 oz. can sliced water chestnuts, drained
1 8 oz. can mandarin oranges, drained
1/2 to 3/4 cup fat-free croutons
4 hard-cooked egg whites, cut up
fat-free Italian dressing
1/2 cup fat-free Baco Bits (optional)

directions:
Wash and drain spinach; then cut up.
Add onions, water chestnuts, and oranges, and toss lightly.
Add croutons and cooked egg whites.
Heat dressing and pour over salad just before serving.
Add Baco Bits*, if desired.

Serves: 6 to 8

<u>**Nutrition per Serving**</u>
Calories	91
Protein	6 grams
Carbohydrate	17 grams
Cholesterol	0 milligrams
Sodium	124 milligrams
Dietary Fiber	3 grams

<u>**Exchanges**</u>
3 vegetable
1/2 meat

*Nutrition analysis without Baco Bits.

GAZPACHO SALAD

AVERAGE - DO AHEAD

---

ingredients:
1/2 cup uncooked rice
2 cups seeded and diced tomatoes
1 cup seeded and diced cucumber
2/3 cup seeded and diced green pepper
1/4 cup chopped onion
1 tbsp. + 2 tsp. red-wine vinegar
2 to 3 tsp. minced garlic
romaine or red-leaf lettuce

directions:
Cook the rice according to package directions, without adding any butter.

In a blender, combine 1 cup of the tomatoes, 1/2 cup cucumber, 1/3 cup green pepper, 2 tablespoons onion, minced garlic and red-wine vinegar.

In a large bowl, combine the rice with the dressing, and toss until thoroughly blended.

Add the remaining tomatoes, cucumber, green pepper and onion, and toss until just combined.

Refrigerate up to 4 hours. Line platter with lettuce and arrange salad on top.

Great served with fat-free tortilla chips or fat-free garlic toast!!

Serves: 4

Nutrition per Serving

Calories	121
Protein	3 grams
Carbohydrate	27 grams
Sodium	198 milligrams
Dietary Fiber	1 gram

Exchanges
3 vegetable
1/2 starch

HONEY-MUSTARD POTATO SALAD

EASY - DO AHEAD

ingredients: 2 lbs. red potatoes, sliced
water
1/2 cup fat-free mayonnaise
1 tbsp. honey
1 tbsp. fat-free Dijon mustard
1 tsp. celery seed
1 garlic clove, minced
1/2 cup chopped red bell pepper
1/2 cup sliced carrot
1/2 cup sliced celery
1/4 cup sliced green onions

directions: Place potato slices in a 4-quart Dutch oven and add enough water to cover. Bring to a boil for 10-12 minutes or until cooked through.
Drain and rinse the potatoes in cold water.
Combine the mayonnaise, honey, mustard, celery seed, and garlic in a large bowl and mix well.
Add the cooked potatoes, bell pepper, carrot, celery and onions, and mix lightly.
Refrigerate until ready to serve.

Serves: 12

Nutrition per Serving

		Exchanges
Calories	50	1/2 starch
Protein	0 grams	1/2 vegetable
Carbohydrate	11 grams	
Cholesterol	0 milligrams	
Sodium	94 milligrams	
Dietary Fiber	0 grams	

SPRING GARDEN SALAD

EASY

ingredients: 1/2 cup cooked asparagus tips
1/2 cup sliced radishes
1/2 cup sliced cucumber
1 cup shredded lettuce
2 tbsp. minced green pepper
4 green onions, minced
1 tbsp. minced parsley
1/4 cup grated fat-free Cheddar cheese
1/4 cup fat-free French dressing

directions: Toss all ingredients together lightly and serve.

Serves: 4

Nutrition per Serving
Calories	54
Protein	5 grams
Carbohydrate	7 grams
Cholesterol	0 milligrams
Sodium	210 milligrams
Dietary Fiber	1 gram

Exchanges
1/2 meat
1 vegetable

VEGETABLE POTATO SALAD
EASY - DO AHEAD

ingredients: 4 medium potatoes, cooked, peeled, sliced
1 7 oz. can whole kernel corn, drained
1/2 cup sliced celery
1/2 cup thinly sliced carrots
1/4 cup sliced radishes
1/4 cup chopped green pepper
1/4 cup chopped onion
3/4 cup fat-free mayonnaise
1 tbsp. sugar
pepper, to taste
1 tbsp. vinegar
2 tsp. prepared mustard

directions: Combine the mayonnaise, sugar, pepper, vinegar and mustard, and blend well.

In separate bowl, combine the cooked potatoes, corn, celery, carrots, radishes, green pepper, and onion. Spoon the dressing over the salad mixture and mix well. Cover and refrigerate until ready to serve.

Serves: 8 to 10

Nutrition per Serving		Exchanges
Calories	109	1 starch
Protein	2 grams	1 vegetable
Carbohydrate	25 grams	
Cholesterol	0 milligrams	
Sodium	191 milligrams	
Dietary Fiber	1 gram	

MARINATED TOMATO SALAD

EASY - DO AHEAD

---

ingredients: 5 large tomatoes, thickly sliced
1 red onion, thinly sliced
1/2 cup chopped fresh parsley (optional)
3/4 to 1 cup fat-free red wine vinegar Italian dressing

directions: Place tomatoes and onions in alternating layers in a serving dish.
Pour salad dressing over vegetables and marinate in refrigerator.
Sprinkle with parsley, if desired, before serving.

Serves: 4 to 6

Nutrition per Serving

Calories	90
Protein	1 gram
Carbohydrate	21 grams
Cholesterol	0 milligrams
Sodium	246 milligrams
Dietary Fiber	2 grams

Exchanges
3 vegetable
1/4 fruit

OUTRAGEOUS CAESAR SALAD

EASY - DO AHEAD

ingredients:
1 head romaine lettuce, torn into bite-size pieces
1 can artichoke hearts, quartered
1 can hearts of palm, sliced
1 1/2 cups cherry tomatoes, halved
1 cup fat-free croutons
1/3 cup fat-free sour cream
2 tbsp. fat-free mayonnaise
2 tbsp. fat-free Parmesan cheese
1 tbsp. red wine vinegar
1 tsp. minced garlic
1/2 tsp. anchovy paste
1/2 tsp. fat-free Dijon mustard
pepper to taste

directions:
Combine sour cream, mayonnaise, cheese, vinegar, garlic, anchovy paste, mustard and pepper, and blend well.
Refrigerate dressing several hours.
Mix lettuce, artichoke hearts, hearts of palm, cherry tomatoes, and croutons in a large bowl.
Toss with dressing and serve.

Serves: 4

Nutrition per Serving
Calories   116
Protein   7 grams
Carbohydrate   23 grams
Cholesterol   0 milligrams
Sodium   454 milligrams
Dietary Fiber   1 gram

Exchanges
3 vegetable
1/2 starch

DR. RICK'S CUCUMBER SALAD

EASY - DO AHEAD

ingredients:
3 cucumbers
1 medium onion
16 oz. nonfat sour cream
3/8 cup sugar
1 tbsp. salt

directions:
Peel the cucumbers and rake sides with a fork.
Slice the cucumber into 1/2-inch pieces.
Thinly slice the onion.
Mix the sour cream, onions, and cucumbers.
Add the sugar and salt.
Marinate vegetables overnight.
Add sugar or salt to taste, before serving.

Serves: 6

Nutrition per Serving

Calories	120
Protein	6 grams
Carbohydrate	25 grams
Cholesterol	0 milligrams
Sodium	1120 milligrams
Dietary Fiber	2 grams

Exchanges
1 starch
1 vegetable
1/4 fruit

Dr. Rick Shaikewitz, Chiropractic Physician,
Chandler, Arizona

SUMMER VEGGIE SALAD

EASY

---

ingredients: 1 cup cauliflower
1 cucumber, cubed
2 large tomatoes, cubed into large pieces
2 green onions, diced
1 lb. can bean sprouts
1 8 oz. can Chinese chestnuts (drained)
sliced red onion
Italian fat-free dressing
fat-free sour cream
fat-free Parmesan cheese

directions: Combine cauliflower, cucumber, tomatoes, green onions, bean sprouts, and chestnuts in a large bowl. Add salad dressing and sour cream, alternately, until of desired coating and taste.
Place sliced onion on top and sprinkle with small amount of fat-free Parmesan cheese.
Great summer salad!!

Serves: 4

Nutrition per Serving

Calories	102
Protein	5 grams
Carbohydrate	22 grams
Cholesterol	0 milligrams
Sodium	131 milligrams
Dietary Fiber	2.8 grams

Exchanges
4 vegetable

ORIENTAL FAT-FREE TURKEY SALAD

EASY - DO AHEAD

ingredients:
1 cup fresh bean sprouts
4 cups sliced fat-free turkey or chicken
2 cups cooked rice, cold
1 cup thinly sliced celery
1/2 cup thinly sliced green onion
3/4 cup fat-free mayonnaise
1/4 cup lime juice
4 tsp. soy sauce
1 tsp. dry mustard
1 tsp. curry powder
1 tsp. garlic powder
3 cups shredded celery cabbage
cherry tomatoes, sliced cucumber

directions:
Rinse and drain bean sprouts.
In a large bowl, combine the turkey or chicken, rice, celery, green onions, and bean sprouts.
Stir together mayonnaise, lime juice, soy sauce, mustard, curry powder, and garlic powder.
Chill the salad and dressing separately.
Just before serving, pour dressing over salad.
Line a large serving platter with shredded cabbage and place the turkey mixture on top.
Garnish the plate with cherry tomatoes and sliced cucumbers.

Serves: 6

Nutrition per Serving		**Exchanges**
Calories	269	3 meat
Protein	25 grams	1 1/2 starch
Carbohydrate	34 grams	1 vegetable
Cholesterol	34 grams	
Sodium	2113 milligrams	
Dietary Fiber	2 grams	

NINE-LAYER SALAD

EASY - DO AHEAD

ingredients:
2 large heads lettuce (iceberg or red leaf)
several ribs celery, thinly sliced
1 Spanish onion, chopped
1 green pepper, chopped fine
1 10 oz. package frozen peas, defrosted
1 cup fat-free mayonnaise
1 pint fat-free sour cream
3 tbsp. sugar
fat-free Baco Bits (optional)
8 oz. fat-free shredded Cheddar cheese

directions:
Using a large, low salad bowl, fill the bowl half-full of torn lettuce.

Top with a layer of celery, followed by a layer of green pepper, onions, and peas.

Mix the mayonnaise and sour cream together and make sure to spread over the entire top of the salad so that it will stay crisp.

Sprinkle 3 large tablespoons of sugar over mayonnaise mixture. Sprinkle Baco Bits on top, if desired.

Sprinkle with grated cheese before serving.

This can be made 3 days ahead and kept refrigerated.

Toss the salad just before serving.

Serves: 12

Nutrition per Serving

Calories	96
Protein	8 grams
Carbohydrate	14 grams
Cholesterol	0 milligrams
Sodium	370 milligrams
Dietary Fiber	2 grams

Exchanges
1/2 starch
1/2 meat
1 vegetable

POTATO SALAD
EASY - DO AHEAD

ingredients: 3 1/2 lbs. potatoes, boiled in skins, peeled and diced
1 8 oz. jar fat-free Miracle Whip dressing
8 hard-cooked egg whites
3 sweet pickles, diced
2 small onions, diced (optional)
1/2 stalk celery, diced
1 oz. pimentos, sliced
pepper to taste
celery seed to taste
2 tbsp. sugar
1/2 tsp. dry mustard
1/8 tsp. red pepper
1 tbsp. flour
1/2 cup fat-free egg substitute
1/2 cup vinegar
1/2 cup water

directions: To prepare dressing, mix sugar, dry mustard, red pepper and flour together. Add egg substitute, vinegar and water in saucepan; cook slowly until dressing is slightly thickened. Put cooked potatoes in large bowl. Add Miracle Whip, egg whites, pickles, onions, celery, pimentos and seasonings. Toss with dressing; garnish with additional hard-cooked egg whites. Best if prepared a day in advance.

Serves: 12

Nutrition per Serving

Calories	165	
Protein	5 grams	
Cholesterol	0 milligrams	
Carbohydrate	35 grams	
Sodium	218 milligrams	

Exchanges
2 starch

HONEY-YOGURT
FRUIT SALAD
EASY - DO AHEAD

---

ingredients:
1 8 oz. carton nonfat plain yogurt
2 tbsp. honey
1 tsp. grated lime peel
3 plums, quartered
2 peaches, sliced
1 pint strawberries
1/2 pint blueberries
1/2 honeydew melon, cut in chunks or balls

directions:
Combine yogurt, honey, and lime peel in a small bowl, blend well, and set aside.
Arrange fruit on a large platter and serve with honey-yogurt sauce.

Serves: 8

Nutrition per Serving
Calories	75
Protein	2 grams
Carbohydrate	18 grams
Cholesterol	1 milligram
Sodium	27 milligrams
Dietary Fiber	2 grams

Exchanges
1 fruit
1/4 milk

ORANGE JELLO MOLD

EASY - DO AHEAD

ingredients: 2 6 oz. packages orange Jell-O (low-calorie, optional)
1 6 oz. can frozen orange juice, undiluted
1 small can crushed pineapple
1 small can mandarin oranges, drained
1 cup boiling water
1 1/2 cups cold water

directions: Dissolve Jell-O in boiling water and stir well.
Add cold water, orange juice, pineapple, and orange segments.
Mix and pour into mold and chill.

Serves: 6

Nutrition per Serving

Calories	81
Protein	2 grams
Carbohydrate	19 grams
Cholesterol	0 milligrams
Sodium	42 milligrams
Dietary Fiber	1 gram

Exchanges
1 1/2 fruit

STRAWBERRY SURPRISE JELLO MOLD

EASY - DO AHEAD

ingredients:
1 6 oz. package strawberry Jell-O (low-calorie, optional)
2 cups boiling water
4 oz. Grape-Nuts
1 10 oz. package frozen strawberries, thawed
1 large banana
1/2 pint fat-free sour cream

directions:
Pour Jell-O in boiling water and cool.
Crush bananas, berries, and Grape-Nuts and add to Jell-O.
Pour 1/2 mixture in a 9x13-inch pan and gel in refrigerator. Spread fat-free sour cream over top half, and the remainder of banana-berry mixture on top.
Refrigerate until set.

Serves: 8

Nutrition per Serving		Exchanges
Calories	125	2 fruit
Protein	4 grams	
Carbohydrate	29 grams	
Cholesterol	0 milligrams	
Sodium	140 milligrams	
Dietary Fiber	4 grams	

PINEAPPLE SLAW

EASY - DO AHEAD

ingredients:
1 20 oz. can pineapple chunks
1/2 lb. shredded cabbage
1/2 lb. shredded carrots
1/2 cup fat-free mayonnaise
2 tbsp. frozen orange juice concentrate, undiluted
pepper to taste

directions:
Drain pineapple, reserving 2 tablespoons juice.
Combine pineapple with cabbage and carrots.
Mix mayonnaise with orange juice concentrate,
reserved pineapple juice, and pepper until well
combined.
Pour dressing over salad mixture. Toss and chill
for several hours.

Serves: 6

Nutrition per Serving

Calories	90
Protein	1 gram
Carbohydrate	22 grams
Cholesterol	0 milligrams
Sodium	162 milligrams
Dietary Fiber	3 grams

Exchanges
1 fruit
1 vegetable

SWEET PEPPER SLAW

EASY - DO AHEAD

ingredients: 1/3 cup fat-free mayonnaise
1 tsp. dry buttermilk ranch salad dressing mix
1 tsp. honey
2 cups shredded red and/or green cabbage
1/2 cup sliced red or green pepper
1 carrot, shredded
1/4 cup sliced celery
1 small apple, chopped

directions: Mix mayonnaise, salad dressing mix, and honey. Add a small amount of water if dressing is too thick.
Cover and refrigerate until ready to serve.
In a large bowl, combine cabbage, pepper, carrot, celery, and apple.
Pour chilled dressing over cabbage mixture, toss to coat, and serve.

Serves: 3 to 4

Nutrition per Serving		Exchanges
Calories	81	1/2 starch
Protein	1 gram	1/2 fruit
Carbohydrate	19 grams	1/2 vegetable
Cholesterol	0 milligrams	
Sodium	241 milligrams	
Dietary Fiber	3 grams	

ITALIAN COLESLAW

EASY - DO AHEAD

ingredients:
1 1/2 cups shredded green cabbage
1 cup shredded red cabbage
1/2 cup shredded carrots
1/2 cup chopped red bell pepper
1/4 cup chopped onion
1/8 cup vinegar
1/2 cup fat-free Italian dressing
1 tbsp. sugar
pepper to taste

directions:
Combine green and red cabbage, carrots, red pepper, and onion. Stir and set aside.
Combine vinegar, Italian dressing, sugar, and pepper in a covered jar and shake well.
Pour dressing over cabbage mixture and mix well.
Cover and refrigerate.

Serves: 4

Nutrition per Serving		Exchanges
Calories	59	1 vegetable
Protein	1 gram	1/2 fruit
Carbohydrate	15 grams	
Cholesterol	0 milligrams	
Sodium	128 milligrams	
Dietary Fiber	2 grams	

FRUIT AND CABBAGE SLAW

EASY - DO AHEAD

ingredients:
4 cups purchased coleslaw mix
1 cup chopped, unpeeled apple
1/2 cup fat-free mayonnaise
1/4 tsp. celery seed
1 11 oz. can mandarin orange segments, drained, reserving 2 tbsp. liquid

directions:
Combine the coleslaw mix and apple in a large bowl.

In a separate bowl, combine the mayonnaise, celery seed, and reserved 2 tablespoons mandarin orange liquid and mix well.

Pour the dressing over the salad and toss to coat well.

Gently fold in the orange segments.

Cover salad mixture and refrigerate until ready to serve.

Serves: 10

Nutrition per Serving

Calories	42
Protein	0 grams
Carbohydrate	10 grams
Cholesterol	0 milligrams
Sodium	91 milligrams
Dietary Fiber	1 gram

Exchanges
1 vegetable
1/4 fruit

CREAMY COLESLAW

EASY - DO AHEAD

ingredients:
2 1/2 to 3 lbs. coarsely shredded cabbage
4 small carrots, finely grated
1 pint fat-free sour cream
3/4 cup fat-free mayonnaise
1/3 cup ketchup
1/4 cup wine vinegar
2 tsp. celery seed
1 1/2 tsp. onion powder
pepper to taste
garlic powder to taste
1 tbsp. sugar

directions:
Mix the cabbage and carrots together.
Combine the remaining ingredients and toss with the cabbage mixture.
Make at least 4 hours in advance, but best if made a day ahead.

Serves: 8

Nutrition per Serving

Calories	99
Protein	3 grams
Carbohydrate	22 grams
Cholesterol	0 milligrams
Sodium	315 milligrams
Dietary Fiber	4 grams

Exchanges
2 vegetable
1/2 starch

MEXICAN CHILI-BEAN COLESLAW

EASY

---

ingredients:
1/2 cup fat-free mayonnaise
1/2 cup bottled taco sauce
2 tbsp. cider vinegar
1 tbsp. sugar
1 tsp. ground cumin
6 cups shredded cabbage
2 large carrots, shredded
3 scallions, thinly sliced
1 15 oz. can red kidney beans, rinsed and drained
3 tbsp. minced jalapeño chilies

directions:
Combine the mayonnaise, taco sauce, vinegar, sugar, and cumin in a large bowl and mix well.
Add the remaining ingredients and toss to coat well.
Refrigerate until ready to serve.
This slaw is best if served the same day, but is just not as crisp if prepared ahead of time.

Serves: 6

Nutrition per Serving

Calories	120
Protein	5 grams
Carbohydrate	24 grams
Cholesterol	0 milligrams
Sodium	468 milligrams
Dietary Fiber	6 grams

Exchanges
1 starch
1 1/2 vegetable

POTATO SALAD WITH PIZZAZZ

AVERAGE - DO AHEAD

ingredients:
1/2 cup nonfat sour cream
2 tsp. dried dill
1 tbsp. lemon juice
1/4 tsp. pepper
1 8 oz. package small new potatoes, quartered
1 yellow or red bell pepper, seeded and chopped
2 cups sliced fresh mushrooms
1 9 oz. package frozen sugar snap peas, thawed

directions:
Combine sour cream, dill, lemon juice, and pepper in a large bowl, and mix well.
Place potatoes in a medium saucepan, cover with water, and bring to a boil. Reduce heat, cover, and simmer 10 to 15 minutes or until tender.
Drain, and rinse potatoes with cold water to cool.
Add cooked potatoes and remaining salad ingredients to dressing and mix well.

Serves: 6

Nutrition per Serving		Exchanges
Calories	74	1 starch
Protein	4 grams	
Carbohydrate	14 grams	
Cholesterol	0 milligrams	
Sodium	18 milligrams	
Dietary Fiber	1 gram	

PASTA SALAD WITH A TWIST

EASY - DO AHEAD

ingredients:
1 lb. fat-free pasta, cooked
2 cups assorted fresh vegetables
1 red or green bell pepper, chopped
2 tbsp. chopped fresh parsley
1 8 oz. bottle fat-free Italian dressing
1 tbsp. fat-free Dijon mustard
1/4 tsp. pepper

directions:
Cook the pasta according to package directions.
Combine the Italian dressing, mustard and pepper, and set aside.
Combine the cooked pasta and remaining ingredients, and mix well with dressing.
Cover and chill thoroughly.

Serves: 6 to 8

Nutrition per Serving		Exchanges
Calories	153	1 1/2 starch
Protein	5 grams	1 vegetable
Carbohydrate	28 grams	
Cholesterol	25 milligrams	
Sodium	360 milligrams	
Dietary Fiber	2 grams	

FRUITED COTTAGE CHEESE

EASY - DO AHEAD

ingredients: 1 cup nonfat cottage cheese
1/2 cup nonfat sour cream
3 tbsp. peach preserves
6 cups cut-up fresh fruit
2 tbsp. Grape-Nuts or fat-free granola
lettuce leaves

directions: Combine the cottage cheese, sour cream, and preserves in a medium-sized bowl.
Arrange the fruit on salad plates lined with lettuce leaves.
Top fruit with 1/4 cup cottage cheese mixture and top with Grape-Nuts or granola.
The fruit and cottage cheese mixture can be prepared ahead of time and refrigerated.
Do not top with cereal until ready to serve.

Serves: 6

Nutrition per Serving		Exchanges
Calories	138	1 1/2 fruit
Protein	7 grams	1 meat
Carbohydrate	27 grams	
Cholesterol	3 milligrams	
Sodium	161 milligrams	
Dietary Fiber	2 grams	

SALAD DRESSING

EASY - DO AHEAD

ingredients:
    2/3 cup nonfat sour cream
    2/3 cup fat-free mayonnaise
    1/4 cup lemon juice
    squirt of anchovy paste
    dash of garlic powder
    dash of pepper
    1 tbsp. red wine vinegar

directions: Combine all ingredients and mix well.

Serves: 6

Nutrition per Serving

Calories	43
Protein	2 grams
Carbohydrate	9 grams
Cholesterol	0 milligrams
Sodium	338 milligrams
Dietary Fiber	0 grams

Exchanges
1/2 starch

CREAMY CAESAR DRESSING

EASY - DO AHEAD

ingredients:
1/2 cup fat-free mayonnaise
3 tbsp. skim milk
1 1/2 tbsp. lemon juice
2 tbsp. fat-free Parmesan cheese
1 small clove garlic, minced
pepper to taste

directions:
Combine all ingredients and blend until smooth. Refrigerate and serve over romaine lettuce with fat-free croutons.

Serves: 4

Nutrition per Serving

Calories	38
Protein	2 grams
Carbohydrate	8 grams
Cholesterol	3 milligrams
Sodium	409 milligrams
Dietary Fiber	0 grams

Exchanges
1/2 starch

CREAMY GARLIC
SALAD DRESSING
EASY - DO AHEAD

ingredients:
1 cup fat-free sour cream
1 1/2 tsp. Dijon mustard
1/2 tsp. grated lemon rind
1/8 tsp. cayenne pepper
2 tbsp. minced parsley
2 tsp. garlic powder

directions:
Combine the sour cream, mustard, lemon rind and cayenne pepper in a bowl, and whisk well.
Stir in the parsley.
Add the garlic powder to the dressing and mix well.
Cover and chill overnight.
Shake the dressing before using.

Yields: 1 cup
Serves: 8

Nutrition per Serving
Calories	27
Protein	2 grams
Carbohydrate	4 grams
Cholesterol	0 milligrams
Sodium	29 milligrams
Dietary Fiber	0 grams

Exchanges
1/4 starch

SPICY GREEN CHILE DRESSING

EASY - DO AHEAD

---

ingredients: 3/4 cup skim milk
2 1/4 tsp. lemon juice
1/3 cup nonfat sour cream
2 tbsp. canned diced green chiles, drained
1 tbsp. chopped fresh cilantro
1/2 tsp. instant minced onion

directions: Combine the skim milk and lemon juice and blend well.
Add all the other ingredients and mix until smooth.

Yields: 1 1/4 cups
Serves: 8

Nutrition per Serving		**Exchanges**
Calories	17	1/4 starch
Protein	2 grams	
Carbohydrate	3 grams	
Cholesterol	< 1 milligram	
Sodium	14 milligrams	
Dietary Fiber	0 grams	

CREAMY PARMESAN DRESSING

EASY - DO AHEAD

ingredients:
1/2 cup skim milk
1/3 cup nonfat sour cream
1/3 cup fat-free mayonnaise
1/4 cup grated fat-free Parmesan cheese
1/2 tsp. dried dill
1/4 tsp. garlic powder
1/4 tsp. dry mustard
pepper to taste

directions:
Combine all the ingredients and blend until smooth.

Yields: 1 1/4 cups
Serves: 8

Nutrition per Serving		Exchanges
Calories	28	1/4 starch
Protein	2 grams	
Carbohydrate	5 grams	
Cholesterol	3 milligrams	
Sodium	157 milligrams	
Dietary Fiber	0 grams	

HONEY YOGURT DRESSING

EASY - DO AHEAD

ingredients: 1 cup plain nonfat yogurt
2 3/4 tbsp. honey
1/4 tsp. ground nutmeg

directions: Blend all the ingredients together until smooth.
Store in a covered jar in the refrigerator and shake
well before using.
Great on fruit salads!!

Yields: 1 cup
Serves: 4

Nutrition per Serving		Exchanges
Calories	33	1/3 milk
Protein	3 grams	
Carbohydrate	5 grams	
Cholesterol	1 milligram	
Sodium	44 milligrams	
Dietary Fiber	0 grams	

FAT-FREE THOUSAND ISLAND DRESSING

EASY - DO AHEAD

ingredients:
1 cup fat-free mayonnaise
1/2 to 3/4 cup chili sauce
2 hard-cooked egg whites, finely chopped
2 tbsp. chopped chives
2 tbsp. minced green pepper
2 tbsp. minced parsley
1 tbsp. sweet pickle relish
1 tbsp. Worcestershire sauce
dash of Tabasco

directions:
Combine all ingredients and refrigerate.
Can be made 2 to 3 days in advance and keeps for several weeks.

Yields: 1 3/4 cups
Serves: 12

Nutrition per Serving		Exchanges
Calories	25	1/4 starch
Protein	< 1 grams	
Carbohydrate	5 grams	
Cholesterol	0 milligrams	
Sodium	291 milligrams	
Dietary Fiber	< 1 gram	

CREAMY JALAPEÑO DRESSING

EASY - DO AHEAD

---

ingredients:
1/4 cup fat-free mayonnaise
1/4 cup fat-free sour cream
1 to 2 tbsp. diced fresh jalapeño pepper
1 to 2 tbsp. skim milk
1/2 tsp. lemon juice
1/8 tsp. onion powder

directions:
Combine all the dressing ingredients and blend well.
Refrigerate at least 1 hour to blend flavors.

Serves: 4

Nutrition per Serving		Exchanges
Calories	27	1/4 starch
Protein	1 gram	
Carbohydrate	5 grams	
Cholesterol	0 milligrams	
Sodium	194 milligrams	
Dietary Fiber	< 1 gram	

MAGNIFICENT
MAIN COURSES

SEAFOOD RICE CASSEROLE

EASY - DO AHEAD

ingredients: 2 cups cooked fat-free rice
1/2 cup green pepper, chopped
1 cup celery, chopped
1/2 cup onion, finely chopped
1 can water chestnuts, sliced and drained
8 oz. fat-free lobster
12 oz. fat-free imitation crab flakes
1 cup fat-free mayonnaise
1 cup tomato juice
1/8 tsp. pepper
1 cup shredded fat-free Cheddar cheese

directions: Preheat oven to 350 degrees.
Combine rice, green pepper, celery, onion, water chestnuts, seafood, mayonnaise, tomato juice, and pepper, and mix well.
Pour into a casserole lightly sprayed with cooking spray. Top casserole with cheese.
Bake 25 minutes at 350 degrees.

Serves: 6

Nutrition per Serving

		Exchanges
Calories:	219	2 starch
Protein	16 grams	2 meat
Carbohydrate	35 grams	
Cholesterol	8 milligrams	
Sodium	1153 milligrams	
Dietary Fiber	2 grams	

EGGPLANT PASTA

AVERAGE - DO AHEAD

ingredients: 1 large eggplant, sliced
1 to 2 cups fat-free bread crumbs or cracker crumbs
onion powder, garlic powder, oregano to taste
1/2 cup fat-free Parmesan cheese
1/2 cup fat-free egg substitute
8 oz. fat-free mozzarella cheese
8 oz. pasta (spaghetti, capellini, etc...)
32 oz. fat-free spaghetti sauce (any flavor)

directions: Preheat oven to 350 degrees.
Cook pasta according to package directions and place in a 9x11-inch baking dish, lightly sprayed with cooking spray.
Cover pasta with a layer of spaghetti sauce; set aside.
Combine bread crumbs, Parmesan cheese and seasonings in a bowl.
Coat eggplant slices with egg substitute, then coat with crumb mixture.
Place eggplant slices on a foil-lined cookie sheet, lightly sprayed with cooking spray, and bake in preheated oven 30 minutes or until tender.
Arrange eggplant slices on cooked pasta, cover with another layer of spaghetti sauce and top with mozzarella cheese.
Return to oven and bake until cheese is melted.

Serves: 4

Nutrition per Serving		**Exchanges**
Calories	335	2 starch
Protein	29 grams	2 meat
Carbohydrate	47 grams	2 vegetable
Cholesterol	18 milligrams	
Sodium	1315 milligrams	
Dietary Fiber	0 grams	

SHRIMP SCRAMBLE

EASY

ingredients:
1 1/2 cups fat-free egg substitute
3 tbsp. skim milk
1 4 1/2 oz. can shrimp, drained
1/4 tsp. pepper
1/2 tsp. prepared mustard
3 bialys, halved

directions:
Combine egg substitute and milk in a medium bowl and mix well.
Stir shrimp into egg mixture; add pepper and mustard and mix well.
Toast bialys and keep warm
Lightly spray a nonstick skillet with cooking spray.
Add egg mixture and cook, stirring lightly with a fork.
When eggs are set and creamy, spoon over bialy halves.
Serve immediately.

Serves: 3

Nutrition per Serving

Calories	167
Carbohydrate	15 grams
Protein	19 grams
Cholesterol	74 milligrams
Sodium	260 milligrams
Dietary Fiber	0 grams

Exchanges

3 meat
3/4 starch

OVEN BAKED SEAFOOD SALAD

EASY - DO AHEAD

ingredients: 1 6 oz. package fat-free lobster
1 8 oz. can crabmeat, drained and rinsed, or 1 cup
frozen imitation crabmeat, thawed and chopped
1 8 oz. can sliced water chestnuts, drained
1 2.5 oz. jar sliced mushrooms, drained
1 cup chopped celery
1/2 cup chopped green pepper
4 hard-cooked egg whites, chopped
1 cup fat-free mayonnaise
2 tbsp. hot fat-free chicken broth
1 tsp. Worcestershire sauce

directions: Preheat oven to 350 degrees.
Lightly spray a 1 1/2-quart casserole with cooking
spray. Combine shrimp, crabmeat, water chestnuts, mushrooms, celery, green pepper, and egg
whites in a large bowl. In a separate bowl, combine
the mayonnaise, Worcestershire sauce, and hot
chicken broth. Pour the dressing over the seafood
and mix well. Spoon into prepared casserole and
bake at 350 degrees for 40 to 45 minutes, or until
hot and bubbly around the edges.

Serves: 6

Nutrition per Serving		Exchanges
Calories	145	1 meat
Protein	9 grams	1 vegetable
Carbohydrate	24	1 starch
Cholesterol	5 milligrams	
Sodium	799 milligrams	
Dietary Fiber	< 1 gram	

CRABMEAT SOUFFLE

EASY - DO AHEAD

ingredients:
8 slices fat-free white bread
2 cups skim milk
1 lb. fat-free crabmeat
1 cup fat-free egg substitute
8 slices fat-free American cheese

directions:
Preheat oven to 350 degrees.
Lightly spray casserole with cooking spray. Place 4 slices bread in casserole. Add one can of crabmeat, and 4 slices cheese.
Alternate layers one more time, ending with cheese.
Beat egg substitute with milk.
Pour egg mixture over top of casserole and bake at 350 degrees for 1 hour.

Serves: 4

Nutrition per Serving
Calories	335
Protein	41 grams
Carbohydrate	39 grams
Cholesterol	14.6 milligrams
Sodium	1439 milligrams
Dietary Fiber	4 grams

Exchanges
2 starch
4 meat
1/2 milk

CHEESE ENCHILADAS

EASY - DO AHEAD

ingredients: 8 fat-free corn tortillas
1 cup fat-free ricotta cheese
2 green onions, chopped
1/2 tsp. ground coriander
3/4 tsp. ground cumin
1/2 tsp. chili powder
1/8 tsp. cayenne pepper
2 tsp. lemon juice
1 cup shredded fat-free mozzarella cheese

directions: Preheat the oven to 350 degrees.
Wrap the tortillas in aluminum foil and warm in the oven for 10 minutes, or until warm and soft.
Remove the tortillas, set aside, and increase oven temperature to 375 degrees.
Combine the ricotta cheese, green onions, coriander, cumin, chili powder, cayenne pepper, and lemon juice in a small bowl and set aside.
Spread 2 tablespoons of the cheese mixture in the center of a tortilla and fold one side over the filling. Fill all the tortillas and place in a baking pan lightly sprayed with cooking spray.
Cover the pan with foil and bake 20 minutes.
Uncover, sprinkle the enchiladas with mozzarella cheese, and bake 5 minutes, or until the cheese is melted.
Serve immediately.

Serves: 8

Nutrition per Serving		**Exchanges**
Calories	137	1 starch
Protein	16 grams	1 1/2 meat
Carbohydrate	16 grams	
Cholesterol	5 milligrams	
Sodium	315 milligrams	
Dietary Fiber	2 grams	

114

CHILI TORTILLAS

EASY - DO AHEAD - FREEZE

ingredients: 12 oz. kidney beans, canned
3 cups fat-free chicken broth
1 large onion, chopped
1 clove garlic, chopped
4 oz. diced green chilies
1 tsp. chili powder
1 tsp. ground cumin
3/4 tsp. dried oregano
1/8 tsp. ground allspice
1/4 tsp. pepper
2 cups fat-free shredded Cheddar cheese
Bottled salsa
8 7-inch fat-free flour tortillas

directions: Combine beans, chicken broth, onion and garlic in a large saucepan. Cook over medium-high heat until onion is soft.

Stir in chilies, chili powder, cumin, oregano, allspice and black pepper. Simmer for 30 to 40 minutes.

Wrap tortillas in foil and heat in 400 degree oven 5 minutes, or until soft.

Spoon bean mixture onto tortillas and top with cheese and salsa, if desired.

Roll tortillas and serve.

Serves: 8

Nutrition per Serving		**Exchanges**
Calories	122	1 starch
Protein	8 grams	1 meat
Carbohydrate	22 grams	
Cholesterol	1 milligram	
Sodium	437 milligrams	
Dietary Fiber	2 grams	

MEATLESS CHILI BEAN TORTILLAS

EASY

ingredients:	6 cups kidney beans, rinsed and drained 8 tbsp. tomato juice 1/2 tsp. ground cumin 1/2 tsp. chili powder 1/2 tsp. chopped garlic 8 fat-free flour tortillas
directions:	Combine the kidney beans, tomato juice, cumin, chili powder, and garlic in a nonstick skillet. Heat over medium heat, 3 to 5 minutes. Heat corn tortillas in a 400 degree oven until soft. Place beans in tortillas and roll up.

Serves: 8

Nutrition per Serving

		Exchanges
Calories	242	3 starch
Protein	13 grams	1 vegetable
Carbohydrate	45 grams	
Cholesterol	0 milligrams	
Sodium	733 milligrams	
Dietary Fiber	11 grams	

VEGETABLE BURRITO CASSEROLE
AVERAGE - DO AHEAD

ingredients:
2/3 cup parboiled fat-free rice
1 to 2 tsp. fat-free chicken broth
1 large green pepper, diced
1 onion, chopped
1 10 oz. package frozen corn, thawed and drained
1 cup salsa-style ketchup
1 cup fat-free Monterey Jack cheese, shredded
8 8-inch fat-free flour tortillas
1 16 oz. can fat-free refried beans
1/2 cup fat-free sour cream
1 tsp. chopped cilantro

directions:
Prepare rice according to package directions, without adding butter or salt.
In a nonstick skillet over medium heat, heat the chicken broth until hot.
Add green pepper and onion; cook until tender. Remove skillet from heat and stir in corn and 1/2 cup salsa-style ketchup. Stir cooked rice and cheese into vegetable mixture. Spread each tortilla with 1/4 cup refried beans. Spoon 1/2 cup rice mixture along center of each tortilla. Roll up tortillas to enclose filling; arrange, seam side up, in glass baking dish. Spoon remaining salsa-style ketchup along center of rolled tortillas; cover with sour cream.
Cover and bake in preheated 400 degree oven 30 minutes or until hot.

Serves: 8

Nutrition per Serving		**Exchanges**
Calories	264	3 bread
Protein	18 grams	1 meat
Carbohydrate	45 grams	
Cholesterol	0 milligrams	
Sodium	801 milligrams	
Dietary Fiber	5 grams	

VEGGIE BAKE
EASY - DO AHEAD

ingredients: 1 eggplant
2 green peppers
1 onion
4 tomatoes
6 to 8 slices fat-free Cheddar cheese (Healthy Choice)
1 16 oz. can crushed tomatoes
fat-free cooking spray

directions: Preheat oven to 350 degrees.
Cut all vegetables in round slices.
Spray 9x12x2-inch pan and layer vegetables.
Put sliced cheese over first layer and continue to layer, sprinkling the top with cheese.
Pour crushed tomatoes over the entire casserole.
Cover with foil and bake 1 hour.
Can be used as a complete meal or a side dish.

Serves: 4

Nutrition per Serving		Exchanges
Calories	178	1 1/2 meat
Protein	15 grams	2 vegetable
Carbohydrate	29 grams	1 starch
Cholesterol	0 milligrams	
Sodium	759 milligrams	
Dietary Fiber	6 grams	

Mary Fluhr, Paradise Valley, Arizona

CRUSTLESS VEGETABLE PIE

AVERAGE - DO AHEAD

ingredients:
1 eggplant, peeled and cubed
1 green bell pepper, chopped
1 onion, diced
2 stalks celery, diced
4 oz. mushrooms, sliced
4 tomatoes, seeded and chopped
1 cup fat-free egg substitute
1/4 tsp. garlic powder
1/4 tsp. oregano
1/4 tsp. pepper
4 oz. fat-free shredded mozzarella cheese
4 oz. fat-free Parmesan cheese

directions:
Preheat oven to 350 degrees.
In a nonstick skillet, lightly sprayed with cooking spray, over medium-high heat, cook eggplant cubes, bell pepper, onion and celery for 10 minutes.
Add mushrooms and chopped tomatoes and simmer on low for 20 minutes. Remove vegetables from heat and allow mixture to cool.
Stir garlic powder, oregano, and pepper into egg substitute and blend well.
Add "sauteed" vegetables to egg mixture and mix well. Place mixture into a 9-inch pie dish, lightly sprayed with cooking spray, and top with cheeses. Bake in a preheated oven for 35 minutes or until a crust forms.

Serves: 4-6

Nutrition per Serving		**Exchanges**
Calories	184	2 meats
Protein	21 grams	4 vegetable
Carbohydrate	24 grams	
Cholesterol	0 milligrams	
Sodium	423 milligrams	
Dietary Fiber	5 grams	

CHEESE, BROCCOLI AND CORN CASSEROLE

EASY - DO AHEAD

ingredients:
2 10 oz. packages frozen chopped broccoli
1 1/2 cups fat-free cottage cheese
1/2 cup fat-free sour cream
1 tbsp. flour
3/4 cup fat-free egg substitute
1 small onion, chopped
1/4 tsp. pepper
1 17 oz. can whole kernel corn, drained
1/2 cup fat-free Parmesan cheese

directions:
Cook broccoli according to package directions just until thawed. Drain well.

Combine the cottage cheese, sour cream, flour, egg substitute, onion and pepper in a large bowl and blend well. Carefully fold in the broccoli and corn and pour mixture into a 2-quart microwave-safe casserole.

Sprinkle Parmesan cheese over top of casserole, cover tightly, and cook on MEDIUM 7 to 10 minutes, or until edges of casserole are set.

Allow casserole to stand 5 minutes before serving.

Serves: 6

Nutrition per Serving		**Exchanges**
Calories	134	1 meat
Protein	12 grams	4 vegetable
Carbohydrate	21 grams	
Cholesterol	1 milligram	
Sodium	369 milligrams	
Dietary Fiber	5 grams	

CHEDDAR MACARONI LOAF

EASY - DO AHEAD

ingredients:
8 ounces elbow macaroni, cooked and drained
2 cups skim milk, scalded
3/4 cup fat-free egg substitute
2 cups fat-free soft white bread crumbs
12 oz. fat-free Cheddar cheese, shredded
1/4 cup minced scallions
2 tbsp. parsley
1/4 tsp. pepper
2 1/2 cups hot fat-free tomato pasta sauce

directions:
Preheat oven to 350 degrees.

Combine all the ingredients except pasta sauce and mix well.

Lightly spray a loaf pan with cooking spray. Pour mixture into pan and bake, uncovered, 1 hour or until firm in center.

Let casserole stand 5 minutes before inverting onto a hot platter.

Spoon pasta sauce over each serving.

Serves: 6

Nutrition per Serving
Calories	257
Carbohydrate	40 grams
Protein	24 grams
Cholesterol	25 milligrams
Sodium	1020 milligrams
Dietary Fiber	2 grams

Exchanges
2 starch
2 meat
1 vegetable

SWISS CHEESE TOMATO BAKE

EASY

---

ingredients:
4 cups fat-free croutons
2 medium tomatoes, sliced
2 cups fat-free shredded Swiss cheese
1/2 cup fat-free egg substitute
1 1/2 cups skim milk
1/2 tsp. paprika
1/2 tsp. dry mustard

directions:
Preheat oven to 350 degrees.
Lightly spray a 9-inch pie plate with cooking spray and arrange croutons in bottom of plate.
Top croutons with tomato slices and sprinkle with shredded Swiss cheese. Combine egg substitute, milk, paprika and mustard in a small bowl, and whisk until lightly beaten.
Pour egg mixture over cheese.
Bake in preheated oven for 40 minutes or until casserole is puffy and browned.
Serve immediately.

Serves: 6

Nutrition per Serving

Calories	211
Carbohydrate	28 grams
Protein	24 grams
Cholesterol	21 milligrams
Sodium	1308 milligrams
Dietary Fiber	1 gram

Exchanges
1 1/2 starch
2 meat
1 vegetable

EGGPLANT CASSEROLE

EASY - DO AHEAD

ingredients:
1 small eggplant
4 medium tomatoes, sliced
2 medium green peppers, chopped
2 medium onions, chopped
garlic powder, onion powder, and pepper to taste
3/4 lb. sharp fat-free Cheddar cheese, sliced or shredded

directions:
Slice unpeeled eggplant 1/4-inch thick and parboil until partially tender.

Place a layer of eggplant slices in a large casserole lightly sprayed with cooking spray.

Add a layer of sliced tomatoes. Fill spaces with a mixture of green peppers and onions.

Add a layer of cheese.

Repeat layers, ending with cheese.

Cover, bake at 400 degrees for 30 minutes.

Uncover casserole, reduce heat to 350 degrees, and cook until the eggplant is tender and sauce is thick and golden (about 30 minutes).

Serves: 6

Nutrition per Serving

Calories	143
Protein	17 grams
Carbohydrate	17 grams
Cholesterol	0 grams
Sodium	540 milligrams
Dietary Fiber	4 grams

Exchanges
3 vegetable
2 meat

VEGETABLE CASSEROLE
AVERAGE - DO AHEAD

---

ingredients:
2 tbsp. Promise Ultra fat-free margarine
1 1/2 cups cooked white rice
2 large onions, chopped
3 cups fat-free vegetable broth
3 tbsp. soy sauce
1/2 tsp. thyme
1 tsp. salt
1/4 tsp. minced garlic
1 large broccoli, cut into florets
2 red bell peppers, cut into strips
1 head cauliflower, cut into florets
2 cups fat-free shredded Cheddar cheese

directions:
Mix margarine, rice and half of the chopped onion, broth, and soy sauce in a 2-quart casserole.
Cover and bake at 350 degrees for 20 minutes.
Remove casserole from oven and stir in thyme and salt.
Spray a nonstick skillet with cooking spray and heat over medium-high.
Add remainder of onion and the vegetables and saute until crisp (about 5 minutes).
Pour over rice mixture in casserole, cover and bake for 10 minutes.
Remove lid and mound Cheddar cheese around edges, and bake for 5 minutes or until cheese is melted.

Serves: 4

Nutrition per Serving		Exchanges
Calories	122	1 starch
Protein	11 grams	1 vegetable
Carbohydrate	19 grams	1 meat
Cholesterol	0 milligrams	
Sodium	977 milligrams	
Dietary Fiber	3.1 grams	

TUNA RICE CASSEROLE

EASY - DO AHEAD

---

ingredients:
2 cans StarKist chunk light tuna in spring water
1 1/2 cups cooked white rice
1/2 cup fat-free shredded Cheddar cheese
1/4 cup fat-free shredded mozzarella cheese
1 12 oz. can evaporated skim milk
1 cup fat-free egg substitute

directions:
Combine tuna, rice and cheese in a large bowl.
In a separate small bowl, blend milk with egg substitute.
Fold egg mixture into tuna mixture.
Place combined ingredients in a 1-quart casserole sprayed with cooking spray.
Bake at 350 degrees until set, about 45 minutes or until toothpick inserted in center comes out dry.

Serves: 8

Nutrition per Serving		Exchanges
Calories	180	2 meat
Protein	24 grams	1 starch
Carbohydrate	17 grams	1 vegetable
Cholesterol	13 milligrams	
Sodium	378 milligrams	
Dietary Fiber	0 grams	

VEGGIE BURGERS

AVERAGE

ingredients:	3 cups cooked lentils
	1 cup fat-free cracker crumbs
	3 egg whites
	1 10 oz. package frozen chopped spinach, thawed and drained
	1/2 cup carrots, cooked
	1/2 cup chopped green onion
	1 cup shredded fat-free Cheddar cheese
	pepper to taste
	8 bialys or 8 slices fat-free bread

directions: Combine lentils, cracker crumbs, egg whites, spinach, carrot, onion, Cheddar cheese, and pepper in a bowl. Shape lentil mixture into 6 patties.

Place patties on a cookie sheet, cover, and refrigerate 2 hours or until firm.

Lightly spray a nonstick skillet with cooking spray and heat over medium-high heat.

Cook patties 3-4 minutes per side, or until browned on each side.

Serve patties on bialys or bread, garnished with lettuce, tomato, ketchup or spicy mustard.

Serves: 6

Nutrition per Serving		**Exchanges**
Calories	258	2 starch
Protein	20 grams	2 vegetable
Carbohydrate	44 grams	1 1/2 meat
Cholesterol	0 milligrams	
Sodium	444 milligrams	
Dietary Fiber	10 grams	

FABULOUS
FISH

CRAB DELIGHT

EASY - DO AHEAD

ingredients: 2 cups fat-free crabmeat (Crab Delights)
1/2 cup fat-free mayonnaise
2 hard-boiled egg whites
2 tbsp. chopped onion
3 chopped celery stalks
pepper and garlic to taste (optional)

directions: Mix all ingredients together.
Serve with fat-free crackers or on lettuce as a terrific lunch salad.

Serves: 4

Nutrition per Serving
Calories	78
Protein	7 grams
Carbohydrate	13 grams
Cholesterol	5 milligrams
Sodium	502 milligrams
Dietary Fiber	.6 grams

Exchanges
1/2 meat
3/4 starch

SCALLOPS PARMESAN

EASY

ingredients: 1 lb. scallops (fresh or frozen)
1/2 cup fat-free Italian dressing
1/3 cup fat-free cracker crumbs
garlic powder and onion powder to taste
1/3 cup fat-free Parmesan cheese

directions: Wash scallops under cold water and pat dry.
Pour Italian dressing into a small bowl.
Combine cracker crumbs, garlic powder, onion powder and Parmesan cheese in a separate bowl.
Dip each scallop in salad dressing, then roll in crumb mixture to coat well.
Place scallops in a circle on a microwave-safe dish and cook on HIGH 2 minutes.
Move outside scallops to center of dish and continue cooking on HIGH 1 to 2 minutes or until scallops are firm.

Serves: 4

Nutrition per Serving

Calories	155
Protein	22 grams
Carbohydrate	12 grams
Cholesterol	44 grams
Sodium	388 milligrams
Dietary Fiber	< 1 gram

Exchanges

2 1/2 meat
1 starch

FRIED SCALLOPS

EASY

---

ingredients:
12 oz. scallops
2 egg whites
1/2 cup matzo meal
1/2 tsp. garlic powder
1/4 tsp. black pepper

directions:
Sprinkle scallops with garlic powder.
Beat egg white with black pepper.
Dip scallops in egg white; then cover with matzo meal.
Spray nonstick skillet with cooking spray and cook scallops over medium-high heat 15 minutes on each side.
Place scallops in glass baking dish, lightly sprayed with cooking spray. Cover with foil, venting sides, and cook in oven 30 minutes at 375 degrees.

Serves: 4

Nutrition per Serving		Exchanges
Calories	149	2 meat
Protein	18 grams	1 starch
Carbohydrate	16 grams	
Cholesterol	28 milligrams	
Sodium	165 milligrams	
Dietary Fiber	1 gram	

Rosy Feldman, St. Louis Missouri

CRAB CAKES

EASY - DO AHEAD

ingredients:
2 cups fat-free crabmeat
1 cup fresh bread crumbs (made from 3 to 4 slices fat-free bread)
1/4 cup fat-free mayonnaise
1 large egg white, lightly beaten
2 tbsp. lemon juice
1 green onion, chopped
1/3 cup red or green bell pepper, chopped
1 tsp. Old Bay seasoning
pepper to taste
1/4 to 1/2 tsp. Tabasco sauce
1/2 cup fat-free bread crumbs

directions:
Preheat oven to 450 degrees.
In a large bowl, stir together crabmeat, fresh bread crumbs, mayonnaise, egg white, lemon juice, onion, bell pepper, Old Bay seasoning, pepper, and Tabasco sauce.
Form into 6 1/2-inch thick patties and roll in dry bread crumbs or cornflake crumbs. Lightly spray a nonstick skillet with cooking spray and heat over medium heat. Add the crab cakes and cook until the undersides are golden, about 1 minute. Carefully turn the crabcakes over and transfer to a baking sheet.
Bake 10 to 12 minutes, or until heated through.

Serves: 6

Nutrition per Serving
Calories	110
Protein	9 grams
Carbohydrate	18 grams
Cholesterol	11 milligrams
Sodium	658 milligrams
Dietary Fiber	2 grams

Exchanges
1 meat
1 starch

SHRIMP AND GREENS

EASY - DO AHEAD

---

ingredients: 1/3 cup tarragon vinegar
1 tbsp. ketchup
2 tbsp. horseradish
1 tsp. mustard
1/4 cup sliced green onion
2 large firm tomatoes, chopped
2 cups canned shrimp, drained
1 head iceberg lettuce, cut into small pieces
Salt and pepper to taste

directions: Combine vinegar, ketchup, horseradish, mustard
and green onion in a small bowl.
Whisk until well blended.
Add tomatoes and shrimp, and mix to coat well.
Put shrimp mixture in refrigerator for several hours.
Arrange 1 cup of lettuce on a small salad plate and
put shrimp mixture on top.

Serves: 8

Nutrition per Serving		**Exchanges**
Calories	71	1 meat
Protein	8 grams	1 vegetable
Carbohydrate	7 grams	
Cholesterol	163 milligrams	
Sodium	135 milligrams	
Dietary Fiber	1 gram	

BAKED SOLE

EASY

ingredients: 1 lb. sole, cut in 6 portions
1/2 tsp. ground pepper
1/2 lb. mushrooms, sliced thin
2 tbsp. fresh parsley, minced
6 tbsp. dry white wine
2 to 3 tbsp. Worcestershire sauce

directions: Preheat oven to 450 degrees.
Arrange sole pieces in a shallow baking dish and sprinkle with pepper.
Cover with sliced mushrooms and sprinkle with parsley.
Mix the wine and Worcestershire sauce together and pour evenly over the sole.
Bake for 12 minutes.

Serves: 6

Nutrition per Serving

Calories	87
Protein	13 grams
Carbohydrate	3 grams
Cholesterol	37 milligrams
Sodium	130 milligrams
Dietary Fiber	0 grams

Exchanges
1 1/2 meat
1 vegetable

SHRIMP PRIMAVERA
AVERAGE

ingredients:
1 cup nonfat cottage cheese
1/2 cup evaporated skim milk
3 oz. fat-free Parmesan cheese
12 large shrimp, shelled and deviened
2 cups sliced mushrooms
1 cup chopped scallion
1 cup diced tomato
2 cups cooked pasta
1 cup broccoli florets
1/2 cup water

directions:
Combine cottage cheese, evaporated milk, and cheese in food processor or blender.

Puree mixture until smooth. Place water in a non-stick skillet and bring to a boil over high heat. Add shrimp and cook until barely pink, about 1 minute. Drain shrimp and set aside.

Lightly spray the skillet with cooking spray and heat over medium-high heat. Add mushrooms and scallions and cook 5 to 8 minutes, until tender. Reduce heat to medium; add tomato and shrimp to skillet. Cook broccoli florets according to package directions (stovetop or microwave).

Add cottage cheese mixture and cooked broccoli florets to skillet and stir gently. Cook until heated through, about 2 to 4 minutes. Pour over cooked pasta and toss.

Serves: 8

Nutrition per Serving

Calories	131
Protein	11 grams
Carbohydrate	21 grams
Cholesterol	17 milligrams
Sodium	239 milligrams
Dietary Fiber	1 gram

Exchanges
1/2 starch
2 vegetable
1 meat

COD FILLETS

EASY

ingredients: 20 oz. cod fillets, cut in 5 portions
1/2 cup nonfat Italian salad dressing
1/8 tsp. pepper
3/4 tsp. paprika
3/4 tsp. dried oregano
1/4 tsp. ground cumin

directions: Sprinkle cod fillets with seasonings.
Baste both sides of cod with Italian dressing.
Cover and refrigerate for 20 to 30 minutes.
Preheat broiler to high heat. Place fish on a rack
and broil 5 to 7 minutes, or until fish flakes easily
when tested with a fork.

Serves: 5

Nutrition per Serving

Calories	104
Protein	20 grams
Carbohydrate	7 grams
Cholesterol	49 milligrams
Sodium	397 milligrams
Dietary Fiber	< 1 gram

Exchanges

2 1/2 meat
1 vegetable

SEAFOOD STUFFED FISH

AVERAGE - DO AHEAD

ingredients:
2 tbsp. Promise Ultra fat-free margarine
3/4 cup fat-free bread or cracker crumbs
1/4 cup chopped green onion
1/4 cup chopped celery
1/4 tsp. minced garlic
4 oz. fresh or frozen shrimp, peeled, deveined, cooked and coarsely chopped
4 oz. fresh or frozen crabmeat or scallops, cooked and coarsely chopped
1 tbsp. parsley
salt and pepper to taste
1 lb. sole fillets, cut into 6 (4 oz.) portions

directions:
Melt 2 tablespoons margarine in nonstick skillet. Add bread crumbs to margarine, and cook over medium heat until crumbs are browned. Set aside. Spray nonstick skillet with cooking spray and cook onion, celery and garlic over medium heat until tender.
Add to bread crumb mixture. Add shrimp, crab or scallops, parsley, salt and pepper to mixing bowl. Place single fillets on double-thickness foil and mound stuffing on top of fillets. Curl edges of foil to form a tray.
Set barbecue grill on medium heat and place fish in foil in center of grill. Cover grill for 20 to 25 minutes, or until fish flakes easily.

Serves: 6

Nutrition per Serving

Calories	120
Protein	22 grams
Carbohydrate	5 grams
Cholesterol	70 milligrams
Sodium	312 milligrams
Dietary Fiber	1 gram

Exchanges
3 meats
1/4 starch

ITALIAN COD

AVERAGE

ingredients:
1 1/2 lb. cod fillets
1 cup onion, chopped
1/2 cup celery, chopped
1/2 cup green pepper, chopped
4 tbsp. fat-free chicken broth
2 tbsp. flour
1 16 oz. can tomatoes
1 tbsp. fresh parsley, finely chopped
1 cup cornflake crumbs
1/4 tsp. oregano
1/2 tsp. garlic powder
1/8 tsp. pepper

directions:
Preheat oven to 375 degrees. Wash fillets, dry well, and cut into serving-size pieces. Arrange fish in a single layer in an 8x12-inch baking dish. In 3 to 4 tablespoons hot chicken broth, cook the onions, celery, and green pepper until they are tender. Remove from heat and blend in flour and pepper. Stir in the tomatoes and parsley and bring to a boil over medium heat, stirring constantly, until the mixture is smooth and thickened. Simmer 1 minute and spoon tomato mixture over the fish. Cover the fish with foil and bake in a preheated oven for 25 minutes. While the fish is baking, combine the cornflake crumbs with oregano and garlic powder. Uncover the fish after 25 minutes and coat with the crumb mixture. Bake, uncovered, 10 minutes longer, or until fish flakes easily.

Serves: 6

Nutrition per Serving

Calories	170
Protein	20 grams
Carbohydrate	19 grams
Cholesterol	41 milligrams
Sodium	357 milligrams
Dietary Fiber	1 gram

Exchanges
2 meat
4 vegetable

FABULOUS FLOUNDER

EASY

ingredients: 1 1/2 lb. flounder
Veggi-Sal

directions: Preheat oven to 350 degrees.
Wash flounder and dry.
Place flounder on foil that has been lightly sprayed
with cooking spray.
Sprinkle Veggie-Sal over flounder.
Bake 30 to 40 minutes, or until fish is evenly
cooked.

Serves: 6

Nutrition per Serving		Exchanges
Calories	86	3 meat
Protein	20 grams	
Carbohydrate	0 grams	
Cholesterol	56 milligrams	
Sodium	86 milligrams	
Dietary Fiber	9 grams	

SOUTHWEST FILLET OF SOLE

EASY

---

ingredients:

2 6 oz. sole fillets
1/2 cup cilantro leaves, finely chopped
1 green onion, chopped
1 to 1 1/2 tsp. diced jalepeño pepper
2 tbsp. lime juice
1/8 tsp. ground cumin

directions:

Stir cilantro, green onion, jalepeño pepper, lime juice, and cumin together in a small bowl.
Spread the seasoning mixture on both sides of the fish fillets and bake in a 350 degree oven for 20 to 30 minutes, or until fish flakes easily with a fork.

Serves: 4

Nutrition per Serving

Calories	79
Protein	16 grams
Carbohydrate	1 gram
Cholesterol	43 milligrams
Sodium	101 milligrams
Dietary Fiber	0 grams

Exchanges

2 meat

FISH PARMESAN

AVERAGE

ingredients: 1/4 cup fat-free egg substitute or 2 large egg whites
1 tbsp. water
1/2 cup fat-free dry bread crumbs (can be made from stuffing croutons)
garlic powder, onion powder, oregano and pepper to taste
1/4 cup fat-free Parmesan cheese
1 lb. cod fillets

directions: Beat the egg substitute with water until combined. Add seasonings to bread crumbs. (If using croutons, crush them to make 1/2 cup crumbs.)
Add the Parmesan cheese to crumbs and mix well. Dip the fish fillets in the egg mixture, then in the crumbs, coating well.
Lightly spray a nonstick skillet with cooking spray and cook fish 5 minutes per side, over medium-high heat.

Serves: 4

Nutrition per Serving		Exchanges
Calories	158	3 meat
Protein	27 grams	2 vegetable
Carbohydrate	11 grams	
Cholesterol	55 milligrams	
Sodium	214 milligrams	
Dietary Fiber	1.5 grams	

PINEAPPLE SHRIMP

EASY

ingredients: 1 lb. shrimp, peeled and deveined
1 large orange
8 oz. crushed pineapple, juice-packed
1/4 cup red onion, minced
1 tbsp. + 2 tsp. jalapeño pepper, diced
3 tbsp. chopped cilantro
1 tbsp. + 2 tsp. lime juice

directions: In a large pot of boiling water, cook shrimp until they turn pink, about 3 minutes. Drain.
Chop the orange segments and combine with pineapple and juice, onion, jalapeño, cilantro, and lime juice.
Arrange some shrimp on each plate and top with pineapple salsa.

Serves: 6

<u>**Nutrition per Serving**</u>

Calories	97	
Protein	12 grams	
Carbohydrate	10 grams	
Cholesterol	86 milligrams	
Sodium	105 milligrams	
Dietary Fiber	1 gram	

<u>Exchanges</u>
1 meat
1/2 fruit

DELECTABLE FISH FILLETS

EASY

---

ingredients: 2 lbs. fish fillets (cod)
4 onions, sliced
1/2 cup fat-free mayonnaise
2 tbsp. Worcestershire sauce
2 tbsp. lemon juice
1/4 cup grated fat-free Parmesan cheese
2 tbsp. chopped fresh parsley

directions: Preheat oven to 350 degrees.
Lightly spray a baking dish with cooking spray.
Add sliced onions and bake until crisp-tender.
Cut fish into individual serving pieces and place on top of onion slices.
Combine mayonnaise, Worcestershire sauce, lemon juice, cheese, and parsley and spread mixture on fish pieces.
Bake in a 350 degree oven for 30 to 40 minutes, or until fish flakes.

Serves: 8

<u>Nutrition per Serving</u>

		<u>Exchanges</u>
Calories	145	2 meat
Protein	22 grams	1/2 starch
Carbohydrate	11 grams	
Cholesterol	49 milligrams	
Sodium	229 milligrams	
Dietary Fiber	2 grams	

TOMATO-FISH PASTA SAUCE

EASY - DO AHEAD

ingredients:	3/4 lb. pasta
	1 14 oz. jar fat-free plain pasta sauce
	3/4 lb. cod fillet, cut in 1" pieces
	1 10 oz. package frozen baby peas, defrosted (optional)
	pepper to taste
directions:	Cook the pasta according to package directions.
	Heat pasta sauce in a saucepan over medium heat, about 3 minutes. Reduce heat to low.
	Stir in fish. Cook 3 minutes, or 5 minutes if using peas. Stir in pepper.
	Serve over hot pasta.

Serves: 8

Nutrition per Serving		Exchanges
Calories	253	2 meat
Protein	13 grams	2 starch
Carbohydrate	46 gram	
Cholesterol	14 milligrams	2 vegetable
Sodium	174 milligrams	
Dietary Fiber	0 grams	

PERFECT PASTA/ RAVENOUS RICE

FAT-FREE FETTUCINI ALFREDO

AVERAGE

---

ingredients:
1 can evaporated skim milk
1 tsp. cornstarch
8 oz. fat-free cream cheese
1/2 lb. sliced mushrooms
6 scallions, chopped
1 lb. fettucini noodles
salt and pepper to taste

directions:
Mix 1 teaspoon cornstarch and 1 teaspoon skim milk in a saucepan.
Add the rest of the skim milk and bring to a boil.
Lower heat to medium and slowly add the cream cheese, stirring constantly.
Simmer mixture until thick.
Add salt and pepper.
Saute mushrooms and scallions in a nonstick skillet sprayed with cooking spray.
Cook fettucini according to package directions.
Toss cooked noodles with sauce.

Serves: 6

Nutrition per Serving

		Exchanges
Calories	373	3 1/2 starch
Protein	19 grams	1 milk
Carbohydrate	70 grams	
Cholesterol	2 milligrams	
Sodium	322 milligrams	
Dietary Fiber	0 grams	

Diane Levy

PASTA CON BROCCOLI

EASY

ingredients:
8 oz. pasta (medium shells)
1 cup skim milk
1 cup fat-free Parmesan cheese
1/2 lb. sliced mushrooms
1 bunch fresh broccoli, chopped
1 8 oz. can tomato sauce
2 tbsp. fat-free butter (or more if needed)
1 to 2 tsp. fresh minced garlic
salt and pepper to taste

directions:
Cook noodles according to package directions and drain well.

Cook broccoli in boiling water until crisp, about 9 minutes. Drain.

In a large nonstick skillet, saute mushrooms and garlic in fat-free butter.

Add cooked broccoli to mushroom mixture with cooked pasta, milk, and tomato sauce.

Stir broccoli mixture and add Parmesan cheese.

Add salt and pepper to taste.

For a little spice, add a dash of cayenne pepper.

Serves: 6

Nutrition per Serving		Exchanges
Calories	141	1/2 milk
Protein	11 grams	1 vegetable
Carbohydrate	24 grams	1 starch
Cholesterol	13 milligrams	
Sodium	433 milligrams	
Dietary Fiber	2 grams	

Michelle Townsend, St. Louis, Missouri

CREAMY SPINACH LASAGNA

AVERAGE - DO AHEAD

ingredients:
8 oz. lasagna noodles (about 9 noodles)
1 onion, chopped
1 8 oz. package mushrooms, sliced
2 10 oz. packages frozen chopped spinach, thawed and squeezed dry
1 tsp. dried oregano leaves
1 tsp. dried basil
1/4 tsp. pepper
1 16 oz. container fat-free cottage cheese
2 egg whites
1/3 c. flour
8 oz. shredded fat-free mozzarella cheese
3 8 oz. cans tomato sauce
1/4 cup fat-free Parmesan cheese, grated

directions:
Cook lasagna noodles according to package directions. In nonstick skillet over medium heat, cook onion, mushrooms and garlic, 5 minutes. Remove from heat; stir in spinach, oregano, basil, and pepper. Set aside. Combine cottage cheese, egg whites, flour and 1 cup mozzarella cheese in food processor or blender; blend until smooth. Preheat oven to 375 degrees. In 9x13-inch baking dish, arrange 3 noodles. Top with 1/2 spinach mixture, half of cheese mixture, and 1/2 tomato sauce. Arrange 3 more noodles, repeat layers. Top with remaining noodles and sprinkle with remaining mozzarella cheese and Parmesan. Bake 45 minutes - let it stand 10 minutes.

Serves: 8

Nutrition per Serving		Exchanges
Calories	253	2 1/2 starch
Protein	21 grams	2 meat
Carbohydrate	40 grams	
Cholesterol	1 milligram	
Sodium	897 milligrams	
Dietary Fiber	3 grams	

CHINESE VEGETABLES
WITH PASTA

EASY

ingredients:
3/4 lb. pasta
3/4 lb. fresh mushrooms, sliced
2 1/2 large carrots
3/4 lb. Chinese pea pods
1 1/2 tsp. ground ginger
1/3 cup soy sauce
1 can + 1 to 2 tbsp. fat-free chicken broth
water
1/4 tsp. crushed red pepper

directions:
Prepare pasta according to package directions.
Slice carrots into thin strips. Remove stems and strings along sides of pea pods.

In a large nonstick skillet over medium-high heat, in hot 1 to 2 tablespoons chicken broth, cook ginger and mushrooms until lightly browned.

Stir in soy sauce and cook, stirring constantly, until mushrooms are tender and liquid is absorbed. Stir in carrots and pea pods and cook about 3 minutes, or until vegetables are tender-crisp.

Add 1 can of chicken broth and 1 cup of water to vegetables and cook over high heat to boiling. Stir in cooked pasta and toss with vegetable mixture. Sprinkle with red pepper.

Serves 6

Nutrition per Serving

Calories	168
Protein	8 grams
Carbohydrate	32 grams
Cholesterol	0 milligrams
Sodium	839 milligrams
Dietary Fiber	0 grams

Exchanges
1 1/2 starch
2 vegetable

PASTA WITH MUSHROOMS

AVERAGE

ingredients:
1 lb. fettuccine or spaghetti
6 large green onions, finely minced (white only)
1/4 tsp. ginger
1 lb. assorted mushrooms, cleaned, trimmed and sliced
2 to 3 tbsp. hot fat-free chicken broth
1 1/4 cups fat-free ricotta cheese
1 1/4 cups fat-free sour cream
1 tbsp. cornstarch
pepper to taste
1/2 cup fat-free Parmesan cheese

directions:
Cook the pasta according to package directions.
In a large nonstick skillet, heat the chicken broth and add the onions, ginger and mushrooms. Cook until the mushrooms become soft. Blend the ricotta and sour cream thoroughly. Blend a small amount of the ricotta mixture with the cornstarch to form a smooth paste.
Spoon the cornstarch mixture into the remaining ricotta mixture and blend thoroughly.
Reduce the heat under the mushrooms to very low.
Stir in ricotta mixture and cook until the sauce is warm, but not hot.
If this mixture gets too hot, it will separate. Season with pepper and spoon over the pasta. Serve with Parmesan cheese.

Serves: 10

Nutrition per Serving		Exchanges
Calories	240	2 starch
Protein	14 grams	1 meat
Carbohydrate	41 grams	1 vegetable
Cholesterol	5 milligrams	
Sodium	86 milligrams	
Dietary Fiber	0 grams	

EGGPLANT, TOMATO, AND PEPPER PASTA

AVERAGE - DO AHEAD

ingredients:
1 1 lb. eggplant
1 tsp. salt
1 cup fat-free chicken broth
3/4 cup chopped onion
3 large garlic cloves, minced
6 ripe Roma tomatoes, chopped
1 red bell pepper, seeded and chopped
1/4 tsp. crushed red pepper flakes
3 tbsp. tomato paste
1 tsp. honey
3/4 lb. pasta

directions:
Peel and dice eggplant and place in a medium bowl and sprinkle with salt.

Toss well and let stand at room temperature 15 minutes to soften.

Bring the chicken broth to a boil in a large saucepan over medium-high heat.

Reduce heat and stir in onion and garlic.

Simmer 3 minutes. Add tomatoes, bell pepper and red pepper flakes. Simmer an additional 10 minutes.

Drain the eggplant and rinse well. Add eggplant, tomato paste and honey to sauce.

Simmer 15 minutes until thickened, stirring occasionally.

Keep sauce warm while the pasta cooks according to package directions.

Serve warm sauce over the pasta.

Serves: 8

Nutrition per Serving
Calories	261
Protein	9 grams
Carbohydrate	54 grams
Cholesterol	0 milligrams
Sodium	398 milligrams
Dietary Fiber	3 grams

Exchanges
2 1/2 starch
2 vegetable

PASTA SHELLS FLORENTINE

EASY - DO AHEAD - FREEZE

---

ingredients:
1 10 oz. package chopped spinach, thawed and well drained
1 cup fat-free shredded mozzarella cheese
1 cup fat-free ricotta cheese
1 egg white, lightly beaten
1 tbsp. fat-free Parmesan cheese
1/4 tsp. ground nutmeg
16 jumbo pasta shells, cooked, drained
1 13 1/2 oz. jar fat-free spaghetti sauce

directions:
Preheat oven to 375 degrees.
Mix spinach, mozzarella cheese, ricotta cheese, egg white, Parmesan cheese and nutmeg until blended.
Fill each shell with a heaping tablespoon of spinach mixture.
Place in 8x12-inch baking dish.
Spoon sauce over shells and cover with foil.
Bake 30 to 40 minutes, or until thoroughly heated.

Serves: 4

Nutrition per Serving

Calories	298
Protein	35 grams
Carbohydrate	33 grams
Cholesterol	10 milligrams
Sodium	907 milligrams
Dietary Fiber	2 grams

Exchanges

1 starch
3 vegetable
4 meat

MEXICAN LASAGNA

EASY - DO AHEAD

ingredients:
1 15 oz. can fat-free chili
1 16 oz. jar fat-free Mexican salsa, drained
1 4 oz. can sliced mushrooms, drained
3/4 cup fat-free Parmesan cheese
1 1/2 tsp. Italian seasoning
1 1/2 cups fat-free cottage cheese
1 1/2 tsp. dried parsley flakes
9 lasagna noodles, cooked
2 1/2 cups fat-free mozzarella cheese

directions:
Preheat oven to 350 degrees.
In a large bowl, combine chili, drained salsa, mushrooms, Parmesan cheese and Italian seasoning.
In a small bowl, stir together cottage cheese and parsley flakes.
Layer cooked noodles, cottage cheese, chili mixture and mozzarella cheese in a 9x9-inch baking dish lightly sprayed with cooking spray.
Repeat layering to make three layers, finishing with cheese.
Bake for 25 to 30 minutes, or until lasagna is thoroughly heated.
Let stand 10 minutes before serving.

Serves: 8

Nutrition per Serving

Calories	300
Protein	35 grams
Carbohydrate	34 grams
Cholesterol	1 milligram
Sodium	948 milligrams
Dietary Fiber	1 gram

Exchanges
2 starch
4 meat

VEGETARIAN LASAGNA

EASY - DO AHEAD

ingredients:
16 oz. fat-free cottage cheese
16 oz. fat-free mozzarella cheese, grated
1/2 cup fat-free egg substitute
2 10 oz. packages chopped frozen broccoli, defrosted and completely drained
1 16 oz. package lasagna
1 32 oz. jar fat-free spaghetti sauce
oregano and pepper to taste

directions:
DO NOT COOK NOODLES.
In a large bowl, mix all the ingredients except noodles and 2/3 of the shredded mozzarella to make the sauce. Lightly spray a 9x13-inch pan with cooking spray. Pour a thin layer of sauce on the bottom of the baking dish.
Add 1/2 of the noodles, 1/2 of the remaining sauce, and repeat, using up the noodles and sauce. Top with remaining mozzarella.
Refrigerate overnight.
Before baking, pour 1 1/2 cups cold water around the edges of the pan, but not in the center.
Bake, lightly covered, at 350 degrees for 1 hour and 15 minutes, then let stand for 15 minutes.
Chopped spinach or sliced zucchini can be substituted for the chopped broccoli. A combination of vegetables can also be used for variety.

Serves: 10

<u>Nutrition per Serving</u>

Calories	160
Protein	21 grams
Carbohydrate	15 grams
Cholesterol	8 milligrams
Sodium	672 milligrams
Dietary Fiber	2 grams

<u>Exchanges</u>
1/2 starch
1/2 vegetable
3 meat

BROCCOLI-CHEESE CASSEROLE

EASY - DO AHEAD

ingredients: 2 packages frozen chopped broccoli
2 cups fat-free cooked rice
3 oz. melted fat-free American or Cheddar cheese

directions: Combine cooked broccoli and rice while hot.
Season with pepper to taste.
Blend in cheese.
Bake, uncovered, in a 350 degree oven for 20 minutes.

Serves: 6

Nutrition per Serving

Calories	119
Protein	6 grams
Carbohydrate	23 grams
Cholesterol	0 milligrams
Sodium	81 milligrams
Dietary Fiber	4 grams

Exchanges

1/4 meat
1 vegetable
1 starch

PASTA GENOVESE

EASY

ingredients:
1 can red kidney beans
10 oz. spaghetti
1 onion, diced
6 cloves garlic, diced
1 cup fat-free beef broth

directions:
Cook pasta according to package directions, without adding butter or salt.
Drain pasta.
Saute onion and garlic in nonstick skillet lightly sprayed with cooking spray.
Mix hot beef broth with cooked onion and garlic and add beans.
Mix with pasta and serve.

Serves: 6

Nutrition per Serving

Calories	276
Protein	11 grams
Carbohydrate	55 grams
Cholesterol	0 milligrams
Sodium	3 milligrams
Dietary Fiber	3 grams

Exchanges
3 1/2 starch

Mike Genovese, St. Louis, Missouri

BAKED ZITI

EASY - DO AHEAD - FREEZE

ingredients:
1 16 oz. box ziti noodles, cooked
1 green pepper, seeded and chopped
1 onion, chopped
1/2 lb. mushrooms
1 26 oz. jar fat-free spaghetti sauce
pepper, garlic powder, oregano to taste
1/2 lb. fat-free mozzarella cheese, shredded

directions:
Lightly spray a nonstick skillet with cooking spray.
Saute green pepper, onion and mushrooms over medium-high heat until tender.
Add seasonings to taste.
Mix cooked ziti noodles with sauce.
Add mozzarella cheese and mix well.
Place ziti combination in a casserole, lightly sprayed with cooking spray, and bake in a preheated 350 degree oven for 30 minutes covered, then 15 minutes more, uncovered, to brown.

Serves: 8

Nutrition per Serving

		Exchanges
Calories	200	1 1/2 starch
Protein	14 grams	1 vegetable
Carbohydrate	31 grams	1 meat
Cholesterol	0 milligrams	
Sodium	554 milligrams	
Dietary Fiber	0 grams	

Janice Rosen, Scottsdale, Arizona

ORIENTAL PASTA
AVERAGE

ingredients: 16 oz. pasta
1 to 2 cups fat-free chicken broth
1/2 cup dry white wine
1 tbsp. minced garlic
1 tbsp. minced ginger
2 carrots, sliced
1 stalk celery, sliced
2 cups broccoli florets
1 yellow squash, sliced
1/2 red bell pepper, sliced
6 mushrooms, sliced
1 green onion, sliced
1 tbsp. cornstarch dissolved in 2 tbsp. water
1 tbsp. light soy sauce
pepper to taste

directions: Cook the pasta according to package directions.
Pour 1 cup chicken broth and wine into a large nonstick skillet and bring to a boil.
Add garlic, ginger, and sliced vegetables to boiling broth. Add more chicken broth as necessary to generously coat the vegetables.
Reduce heat to medium and continue to cook vegetables until tender.
Add cornstarch and water mixture to skillet to thicken sauce.
Toss with pasta and serve.

Serves: 12

Nutrition per Serving
Calories	178
Protein	7 grams
Carbohydrate	35 grams
Cholesterol	0 milligrams
Sodium	100 milligrams
Dietary Fiber	3 grams

Exchanges
2 starch
1 vegetable

COLD PASTA PRIMAVERA

EASY - DO AHEAD

ingredients: 6 oz. rigatoni
2 cups broccoli florets
2 cups cauliflower florets
2 cups chopped red bell pepper
2 cup tomato juice
2 tsp. leaf oregano, crumbled
2 tsp. leaf basil, crumbled
1 tsp. garlic powder

directions: Cook pasta according to package directions.
Add broccoli and cauliflower during last 5 minutes of cooking pasta.
Drain, rinse, and transfer to a bowl.
Add pepper and chill.
Combine tomato juice, oregano, basil and garlic powder.
Toss with pasta.

Serves: 8

Nutrition per Serving
Calories   69
Protein   3 grams
Carbohydrate   15 grams
Cholesterol   7 milligrams
Sodium   233 milligrams
Dietary Fiber   3 grams

Exchanges
1 vegetable
1/2 starch

CHILI RICE

EASY - DO AHEAD

ingredients:
2 cups cooked rice
1 15 oz. can fat-free chili
1 6 oz. can vegetable juice
3 cups frozen mixed vegetables, thawed and drained
sliced green onions
4 tbsp. fat-free sour cream
1 cup fat-free shredded Cheddar cheese

directions:
In a large saucepan, combine chili, vegetable juice, and mixed vegetables.
Bring to a boil, cover, and simmer over low heat for 5 minutes.
Serve over rice, and top with sliced green onions, sour cream, and cheese.

Serves: 4

Nutrition per Serving		Exchanges
Calories	329	3 starch
Protein	21 grams	1 meat
Carbohydrate	57 milligrams	2 vegetable
Cholesterol	0 milligrams	
Sodium	870 milligrams	
Dietary Fiber	10 grams	

MEXICAN RICE

EASY

---

ingredients;
1 small onion
1 small green pepper, seeded and chopped
1 10 oz. package frozen corn, thawed
1 cup + 1 to 2 tbsp. fat-free chicken broth
1 cup mild salsa
1 1/2 cups fat-free Minute Instant Rice
1/2 cup shredded fat-free Cheddar cheese

directions:
In a large nonstick skillet over medium heat, heat 1 to 2 tablespoons chicken broth.
Add onion and green pepper to hot broth and cook until tender.
Add corn, remaining 1 cup chicken broth, and salsa.
Bring combined ingredients to a boil.
Stir in rice, cover and remove from heat.
Let stand for 5 minutes and fluff with a fork.
Sprinkle rice casserole with cheese, cover, and let stand 2 minutes or until cheese melts.

Serves: 6

Nutrition per Serving		Exchanges
Calories	151	1 1/2 starch
Protein	6 grams	1 vegetable
Carbohydrate	31 grams	
Cholesterol	0 milligrams	
Sodium	397 milligrams	
Dietary Fiber	2 grams	

LENTIL RICE

EASY

ingredients:
1 small onion, chopped
2 cups fat-free rice
1 tsp. cinnamon
1 6 oz. can tomato sauce
2 cups fat-free beef broth
1 cup lentils
3 cups water
1 cup raisins

directions:
Lightly spray a nonstick skillet with cooking spray and heat.
Add onion and saute until soft.
Stir in rice, cinnamon, tomato sauce or paste, bouillon cubes, lentils and water.
Stir well.
Bring to a boil, cover, and simmer until rice is done, about 45 minutes.
Stir in raisins and heat through.

Serves: 6

Nutrition per Serving
Calories	345
Protein	8 grams
Carbohydrate	77 grams
Cholesterol	0 milligrams
Sodium	623 milligrams
Dietary Fiber	7 grams

Exchanges
2 vegetable
1 fruit
3 starch

Cathy Traver, Missoula, Montana

VIGOROUS
VEGETABLES

SWEET AND SOUR RED CABBAGE

EASY - DO AHEAD

ingredients:
- 1 small onion, chopped fine
- 2 small apples, diced
- 4 cups red cabbage, chopped
- 1/8 tsp. ginger
- 1/2 tsp. nutmeg
- 1/8 tsp. lemon juice
- 2 tbsp. vinegar
- sugar or sugar substitute to taste
- salt & pepper to taste

directions

Using a large saucepan, cook onion in small amount of chicken or vegetable broth until tender.
Add remaining ingredients and cook, covered, until vegetables are tender.
Stir occasionally.

Serves: 6

Nutrition per Serving		**Exchanges**
Calories	50	1/2 fruit
Protein	0 grams	1 vegetable
Carbohydrate	12 grams	
Cholesterol	0 milligrams	
Sodium	9 milligrams	
Dietary Fiber	2 grams	

Tracy Ann Tallent, Tucson, Arizona

CARROT TZIMMIS

EASY - DO AHEAD - FREEZE

ingredients:
12 oz. canned yams, sliced and drained
3 cups sliced carrots, parboiled
8 large pitted prunes
1/2 cup crushed pineapple with juice
1/3 cup brown sugar
1/3 cup orange juice concentrate
1/4 cup sherry wine

directions:
Preheat oven to 300 degrees.
Combine all the ingredients in a casserole lightly sprayed with cooking spray.
Cover casserole and bake 3 to 4 hours.
Casserole can be made ahead and frozen.
Cover when reheating.

Serves: 6

Nutrition per Serving		**Exchanges**
Calories	179	2 fruit
Protein	2 grams	1 vegetable
Carbohydrate	44 grams	1/2 starch
Cholesterol	0 milligrams	
Sodium	59 milligrams	
Dietary Fiber	4 grams	

CAULIFLOWER PUDDING
AVERAGE - DO AHEAD

ingredients: 1 small head cauliflower, trimmed and chopped
1 clove garlic, minced
1 lb. can low-sodium chopped tomatoes, drained
1/4 tsp. ground ginger
1/8 tsp. black ground pepper
cayenne pepper, to taste
1 1/2 tbsp. flour
1/2 cup plain nonfat yogurt
1 1/2 tbsp. shredded fat-free Swiss cheese

directions: Boil cauliflower in a heavy, covered saucepan and cook for 5 minutes or until barely tender. Drain well.
Preheat the oven to 375 degrees.
Combine the garlic, tomatoes, ginger, pepper, cayenne pepper, and cauliflower in a nonstick skillet and cook, covered, over moderate heat for 10 minutes or until the cauliflower is tender.
Boil away any remaining liquid by raising the heat to high and uncovering the skillet.
Blend the cauliflower mixture in a blender or food processor in several batches for 30 seconds each.
Stir together the flour, yogurt, cheese, and cauliflower mixture.
Transfer the mixture to an ungreased 9-inch pie plate and bake 20 minutes or until the top is crust.

Serves: 4

Nutrition per Serving
Calories	80
Protein	5 grams
Carbohydrate	14 grams
Cholesterol	0 milligrams
Sodium	80 milligrams
Dietary Fiber	2 grams

Exchanges
1/2 meat
2 vegetable

TANGY MUSTARD CAULIFLOWER

EASY

---

ingredients:

1 medium head cauliflower
1/2 cup fat-free mayonnaise
1 to 1 1/2 tsp. prepared mustard
1 green onion, sliced
2 oz. shredded fat-free Cheddar or American cheese

directions:

Place the cauliflower in a large saucepan, cover with water, and boil over high heat until crisp and tender.
Drain well.
Combine mayonnaise, mustard, and onion in a small bowl and spread over the cauliflower (on serving platter). Sprinkle with cheese, cover, and let stand a few minutes until cheese is melted.

Serves: 4

Nutrition per Serving

Calories	66
Protein	6 grams
Carbohydrate	10 grams
Cholesterol	0 milligrams
Sodium	352 milligrams
Dietary Fiber	2 grams

Exchanges
2 vegetable

CORN PUDDING

EASY - DO AHEAD

ingredients:
1/4 cup fat-free egg substitute
1 large egg white
1 cup skim milk
2 tbsp. flour
1/4 tsp. baking powder
1/8 tsp. pepper
1 1/3 cups frozen whole-kernel corn
2 green onions, including tops, chopped fine
2 tsp. fat-free grated Parmesan cheese

directions:
Preheat the oven to 350 degrees.

Stir the egg substitute, egg white, milk, flour, baking powder, and pepper together in a bowl.

Add the corn, green onions, and cheese and mix well.

Lightly spray a 9-inch pie plate with cooking spray; then add the corn mixture and set the pie plate in a shallow baking dish.

Add enough hot water to the baking dish to come halfway up the sides of the pie plate.

Bake, uncovered, for 1 to 1 1/4 hours or until a toothpick inserted in the center comes out clean. The pudding should be golden and puffy.

Serves: 4

Nutrition per Serving

Calories	91
Protein	6 grams
Carbohydrate	17 grams
Cholesterol	1 milligram
Sodium	101 milligrams
Dietary Fiber	1 gram

Exchanges
1/2 milk
1/2 starch

TANGY GREEN BEANS

EASY

ingredients: 2 cups frozen cut green beans or cut fresh green beans
1/4 cup hot fat-free chicken broth
3 tbsp. sliced green onions
1/4 tsp. cinnamon
pepper to taste
2 tbsp. ketchup

directions: Combine the green beans, chicken broth, onions, cinnamon, and pepper in a medium saucepan and bring to a boil.
Reduce heat and simmer, covered, until the beans are tender (6 to 7 minutes for frozen beans or about 15 minutes for fresh).

Serves: 4

Nutrition per Serving		**Exchanges**
Calories	31	1 vegetable
Protein	1 gram	
Carbohydrate	7 grams	
Cholesterol	0 milligrams	
Sodium	136 milligrams	
Dietary Fiber	1 gram	

MUSHROOMS DELUXE

EASY

ingredients: 6 medium mushrooms, sliced
2 cups frozen peas
1 cup water
3 green onions, chopped
1 tbsp. low-sodium soy sauce

directions: Bring 1 cup water to a boil and add peas.
Cook peas 5 minutes.
Drain well.
Saute mushrooms and onions in nonstick pan sprayed with cooking spray, until tender.
Toss mushrooms with soy sauce, green onions, and peas.

Serves: 4

Nutrition per Serving

Calories	70
Protein	5 grams
Carbohydrate	12 grams
Cholesterol	0 milligrams
Sodium	202 milligrams
Dietary Fiber	3.5 grams

Exchanges
1 starch

POTATO BOATS

EASY - DO AHEAD

ingredients: 6 baking potatoes
4 oz. fat-free cream cheese, softened
1 8 oz. can peas, drained
2 tbsp. skim milk
2 tbsp. onion
salt and pepper to taste

directions: Preheat oven to 450 degrees.
Bake potatoes for 1 hour or until tender.
Cut each potato in half and scoop out pulp, leaving 1/4-inch shell.
Combine potato, cream cheese, and milk; beat until smooth.
Add peas, salt, and pepper and blend into mixture.
Fill potato skins with mixture.
Bake in 375 degree oven on cookie sheet for 20 minutes.

Serves: 6

Nutrition per Serving		Exchanges
Calories	190	2 1/2 starch
Protein	7 grams	
Carbohydrate	38 grams	
Cholesterol	2 milligrams	
Sodium	205 milligrams	
Dietary Fiber	4 grams	

TWO-TIME POTATOES

EASY - DO AHEAD

ingredients: 3 large potatoes
1/3 cup skim milk
1 1/2 tbsp. Promise Ultra fat-free margarine
1 1/2 tbsp. fat-free Parmesan cheese, grated
1/8 tsp. pepper

directions: Pierce potatoes with a fork, then place in pre-heated 400 degree oven.
Bake 1 hour.
Cool slightly. Cut potatoes in half, scoop out pulp, and mash.
Add milk, pepper and 1/2 the margarine to mashed potatoes. Beat until smooth.
Scoop potato mixture into shells and sprinkle with Parmesan cheese. Arrange potatoes on ungreased baking sheet.
Bake for 20 minutes, then broil 1 to 2 minutes, until browned.

Serves: 3

Nutrition per Serving		Exchanges
Calories	164	1 1/2 starch
Protein	4 grams	1/2 milk
Carbohydrate	35 grams	
Cholesterol	0 milligrams	
Sodium	87 milligrams	
Dietary Fiber	3 grams	

BAKED POTATO CHIPS

EASY - DO AHEAD

---

ingredients: Potatoes, leave skin on

directions: Slice potatoes 1/8-inch thick.
Generously spray a cookie sheet with cooking spray.
Place sliced potatoes in a single layer on cookie sheet and bake for 20 to 25 minutes at 450 degrees.

Nutrition per Serving

Calories	145 (per potato)
Protein	3 grams
Carbohydrate	33 grams
Cholesterol	0 milligrams
Sodium	7 milligrams
Dietary Fiber	3 grams

Exchanges

1 3/4 starch

PINEAPPLE SWEET POTATOES

EASY - DO AHEAD

ingredients:
6 medium sweet potatoes
3/4 cup fat-free egg substitute
1/2 cup brown sugar
crushed corn flakes
1/4 cup Promise Ultra fat-free margarine
1 16 oz. can crushed pineapple

directions:
Boil sweet potatoes until soft and peel.
Mash potatoes and add brown sugar, margarine, egg substitute, and pineapple. Beat well.
Lightly spray a casserole with cooking spray.
Place potato mixture in casserole and top with cornflake crumbs.
Bake 50 minutes at 350 degrees.

Serves: 6

<u>**Nutrition per Serving**</u>
Calories	239
Protein	5 grams
Carbohydrate	51 grams
Cholesterol	0 milligrams
Sodium	174 milligrams
Dietary Fiber	3 grams

<u>**Exchanges**</u>
1 starch
1/2 meat
2 fruit

SWEET POTATO CASSEROLE

EASY - DO AHEAD

ingredients:
2 large cans sweet potatoes, drained
2 8 1/2 oz. cans crushed pineapple with syrup
2/3 cup firmly packed brown sugar
1/2 cup golden sherry
miniature marshmallows

directions:
Mash sweet potatoes in a bowl.
Add crushed pineapple with syrup.
Blend in the brown sugar and sherry until the mixture is light and fluffy.
Spoon potato mixture into a casserole lightly sprayed with cooking spray.
Cover the entire surface with miniature marshmallows and bake in a 350 degree oven for 45 minutes.

Serves: 8

Nutrition per Serving

Calories	292
Protein	2 grams
Carbohydrate	70 grams
Cholesterol	0 milligrams
Sodium	70 milligrams
Dietary Fiber	2 grams

Exchanges
1 starch
3 1/2 fruit

POTATO KUGEL

EASY - DO AHEAD

ingredients: 8 medium baking potatoes, peeled and grated
2 onions, grated
2 carrots, grated
1 1/2 cups fat-free egg substitute
2 tsp. salt-free seasoning
1/4 tsp. pepper
7 to 8 tbsp. matzo meal

directions: Preheat oven to 400 degrees.
Beat egg substitute and combine with well-drained grated onions, carrots, potatoes, and seasonings. Add matzo meal and mix well.
Place potato mixture into a lightly sprayed 8x11-inch baking dish and bake in a preheated oven for 30 minutes.
Reduce temperature to 350 degrees, and bake an additional 30 to 45 minutes.

Serves: 6

Nutrition per Serving

		Exchanges
Calories	258	3 starch
Protein	11 grams	1 vegetable
Carbohydrate	53 grams	
Cholesterol	0 milligrams	
Sodium	119 milligrams	
Dietary Fiber	3 grams	

CREAMY MASHED POTATOES

EASY - DO AHEAD

---

ingredients:
6 potatoes, peeled and cut into 2-inch pieces
16 oz. nonfat sour cream
2 tbsp. fat-free Parmesan cheese
1 tbsp. garlic powder
salt and pepper to taste
2 tbsp. chives (optional)
paprika (optional)

directions:
Place 6 cups of water and 1 teaspoon salt into a large pot and bring to a boil over high heat.
Place potato pieces into boiling water and reduce heat to medium.
Cook potatoes over medium-high heat about 20 minutes, or until easily pierced with a fork.
Place cooked potatoes into a colander and drain well.
In a large mixing bowl, combine cooked potatoes and remaining ingredients, and mix on medium speed with hand mixer until smooth.
Preheat oven to 350 degrees.
Place potato mixture into a large casserole dish and sprinkle top with paprika, if desired.
Cook potatoes at 350 degrees for about 20 minutes, or until potatoes start to bubble on the sides.

Serves: 6 to 8

Nutrition per Serving

		Exchanges
Calories	179	2 starch
Protein	8 grams	1 vegetable
Carbohydrate	36 grams	
Cholesterol	0 milligrams	
Sodium	75 milligrams	
Dietary Fiber	1 gram	

Diane Levy

TWICE-BAKED POTATOES, COTTAGE STYLE

EASY - DO AHEAD

ingredients:
4 medium potatoes
1 cup fat-free cottage cheese
1/2 cup skim milk
1 tbsp. diced onion
1/2 tsp. salt
1/2 tsp. pepper
1/2 tsp. paprika
1/2 tsp. dried parsley flakes

directions:
Gently scrub potatoes under cold water with vegetable brush to clean.

Pierce each potato in several places with tines of fork.

Bake at 400 degrees for 45 minutes or until tender.

Cut hot potatoes in half lengthwise.

Scoop out potato, leaving skins intact for re-stuffing.

With wire whisk, beat potato with remaining ingredients, except paprika and parsley flakes, until fluffy. Pile mixture back into skins.

Sprinkle with paprika and parsley flakes.

Bake 10 minutes more, or until just golden.

Serves: 4

Nutrition per Serving

Calories	172
Protein	11 grams
Carbohydrate	31 grams
Cholesterol	5 milligrams
Sodium	473 milligrams
Dietary Fiber	2 grams

Exchanges
1 1/4 starch
1 milk

POTATO CASSEROLE

EASY - DO AHEAD

---

ingredients: Red baking potatoes (1 per 2 people)
1 package nonfat American cheese
1 to 2 jumbo onions, sliced
fat-free butter or cooking spray
salt, pepper, garlic powder

directions: Boil whole potatoes in water 30 minutes or until tender. Let potatoes cool.
Slice potatoes 1/4-inch thick (skin on).
Spray 8x13-inch baking dish with cooking spray.
Layer potatoes on bottom of dish. Spray with cooking spray or brush with melted, fat-free butter.
Sprinkle with salt, pepper and garlic powder to taste.
Top with slices of fat-free American cheese and onions.
Repeat layers.
Bake in 350 degree oven for 20 to 30 minutes or until hot.
Skim milk may be added, if needed, for moistness.

Serves: 8

Nutrition per Serving

Calories	200
Protein	11 grams
Carbohydrate	38 grams
Cholesterol	0 milligrams
Sodium	229 milligrams
Dietary Fiber	4 grams

Exchanges

1 1/2 starch
1/2 meat
2 vegetable

Michelle Townsend, St. Louis Missouri

SUPER STUFFED POTATOES

EASY

ingredients:
4 large baking potatoes
1 16 oz. carton fat-free sour cream
1 cup shredded fat-free Cheddar cheese
1 10 oz. package frozen chopped spinach
pepper to taste

directions:
Prick the potatoes with a fork.
Preheat the oven to 450 degrees.
Bake potatoes 1 hour or until easily pierced with a fork.
Cook the spinach according to package directions and drain well.
Reduce the oven temperature to 400 degrees.
Cut the cooked potatoes in half and scoop out the inside, leaving a 1/4-inch shell.
Mash the cooked potatoes with the sour cream.
Stir in the cooked spinach and pepper.
Spoon the potato-spinach mixture back into the shells and top with shredded Cheddar cheese.
Bake 10 to 15 minutes, or until cheese is well melted on top.

Serves: 4

Nutrition per Serving
Calories	329
Protein	28 grams
Carbohydrate	52 grams
Cholesterol	0 milligrams
Sodium	691 milligrams
Dietary Fiber	4 grams

Exchanges
2 starch
2 meat
4 vegetable

SCRUMPTIOUS MASHED POTATOES

EASY

ingredients: 2 lbs. baking potatoes, cut in chunks (peeled or unpeeled)
1 envelope dry onion soup mix
3/4 cup skim milk, heated to boiling
1/2 cup fat-free sour cream

directions: In a 3-quart saucepan, cover potatoes with water. Bring to a boil over high heat.
Reduce heat to low and simmer 20 minutes or until potatoes are very tender; drain.
Return potatoes to saucepan and mash.
Mix onion soup mix with hot milk and sour cream, and stir into mashed potatoes until smooth and fluffy.

Serves: 8

Nutrition per Serving
Calories   129
Protein   4 grams
Carbohydrate   27 grams
Cholesterol   0 milligrams
Sodium   464 milligrams
Dietary Fiber   0 grams

Exchanges
1 1/2 starch

"AU GRATIN" POTATOES
EASY - DO AHEAD

ingredients: 5 medium-size all-purpose potatoes, peeled
1 1/2 cups nonfat cottage cheese
1/4 cup fat-free egg substitute
pepper to taste
2 whole green onions, chopped
1 cup shredded fat-free Cheddar cheese

directions: Cover the peeled potatoes with enough water to cover, in a medium saucepan. Cook over medium-high heat 20 to 25 minutes or until tender.
Drain the potatoes, cool, and slice thin.
Preheat the oven to 375 degrees.
Combine the cottage cheese, egg substitute, and pepper and blend until smooth.
Lightly spray a shallow casserole dish with cooking spray and place 1/3 of the potatoes in a single layer in the casserole.
Spread 1/2 of the cottage cheese mixture on top of the potatoes and sprinkle with 1/3 of the green onions and Cheddar cheese.
Add another 1/3 of the potatoes and spread with the remaining cottage cheese mixture.
Top with the remaining potatoes and sprinkle with the remaining green onions and Cheddar cheese. Bake the casserole for 30 to 40 minutes or until golden.

Serves: 4

Nutrition per Serving

Calories	303
Protein	31 grams
Carbohydrate	41 grams
Cholesterol	7 milligrams
Sodium	870 milligrams
Dietary Fiber	1 gram

Exchanges
2 starch
2 meat
1 milk

POTATO LATKES

EASY - DO AHEAD - FREEZE

ingredients: 4 large potatoes, cut in quarters
1 large onion, cut in quarters
1 cup fat-free egg substitute
1/2 cup flour

directions: Combine all ingredients in a food processor or blender, and blend until well-mixed, but not chopped too fine.

Lightly spray a nonstick skillet with cooking spray and heat over medium-high heat.

Drop potato mixture by tablespoons into the hot skillet, and cook on both sides until brown and crisp.

Cooked latkes can be frozen and reheated at 450 degrees for 7 to 10 minutes.

Serves: 8

Nutrition per Serving

Calories	121
Protein	6 grams
Carbohydrate	25 grams
Cholesterol	0 milligrams
Sodium	55 milligrams
Dietary Fiber	2 grams

Exchanges
1 1/2 starch

CHILI POTATOES

EASY - DO AHEAD

ingredients: 6 large baking potatoes
2 15 oz. cans fat-free chili
1 1/2 cups fat-free shredded Cheddar cheese
1 1/2 cups fat-free sour cream
3/4 cup chopped green onion (optional)

directions: Wash potatoes, but do not dry.
Pierce potatoes and microwave on HIGH 25 minutes, or until cooked through.
Turn potatoes halfway through cooking.
Remove potatoes from oven.
Heat chili in a covered microwave-safe bowl, on HIGH 6 to 8 minutes, or until heated through. Stir halfway through cooking time.
Cut potatoes in half, lightly mash in shells, and arrange on serving platter.
Divide chili evenly among potato halves and sprinkle with cheese.
Cook on HIGH 2 to 4 minutes, or until cheese is melted. Top each potato with 1 tablespoon sour cream and 1/2 tablespoon chopped green onions, if desired.

Serves: 6

Nutrition per Serving		Exchanges
Calories	334	3 1/2 starch
Protein	23 grams	2 meat
Carbohydrate	53 grams	
Cholesterol	0 milligrams	
Sodium	635 milligrams	
Dietary Fiber	7 grams	

CHEESY SEAFOOD POTATOES

EASY - DO AHEAD

ingredients:
4 8 oz. baking potatoes
6 oz. crabmeat, or imitation crab flakes
pepper to taste
salt substitute to taste
4 tbsp. fat-free sour cream
1/2 cup chopped green onions
1 cup fat-free shredded Cheddar cheese

directions:
Rinse potatoes, but do not dry.

Pierce each potato and microwave 18 to 22 minutes on HIGH. Rotate potatoes halfway through cooking time.

Cool potatoes for 5 minutes; then cut a small piece off the top of each potato.

Scoop the potato into a bowl, leaving a 1/4-inch shell. Mash the potatoes well with sour cream and seasonings.

Add chopped green onions, 3/4 cup cheese, 1/2 cup crabmeat, and mix well.

Spoon the potato-crab mixture back into the shells and top with the remaining crabmeat.

Sprinkle cheese evenly over each potato.

Cook potatoes on a microwave-safe platter on HIGH 2 to 3 minutes, or until cheese melts and potatoes are hot.

Serves: 4

Nutrition per Serving

Calories	234
Protein	16 grams
Carbohydrate	40 grams
Cholesterol	4 milligrams
Sodium	486 milligrams
Dietary Fiber	4 grams

Exchanges
2 1/2 starch
1 meat

SWEET AND TANGY SWEET POTATOES

EASY - DO AHEAD

ingredients:
2 lbs. fresh sweet potatoes
1/2 cup orange juice
1/2 cup brown sugar
1/2 tsp. cinnamon

directions:
Wash sweet potatoes, but keep damp.
Pierce skin several times and wrap each potato in a paper towel.
Cook potatoes in microwave on HIGH 4 to 6 minutes, or until the potatoes are soft.
Allow the potatoes to cool, then peel and cut into thick slices.
Place potato slices in a baking dish.
Mix the orange juice, brown sugar, and cinnamon together and pour over the sweet potatoes.
Cover with a paper towel and cook on HIGH 5 to 6 minutes, until well heated.

Serves: 6

Nutrition per Serving		Exchanges
Calories	199	1 starch
Protein	2 grams	2 fruit
Carbohydrate	49 grams	
Cholesterol	0 milligrams	
Sodium	18 milligrams	
Dietary Fiber	0 grams	

GRILLED POTATOES
WITH ONIONS

EASY

---

ingredients: 3 potatoes, sliced
1 large Vidalia onion, diced
cooking spray

directions: Spray baking dish with cooking spray.
Spread one layer potatoes and onions in baking dish.
Spray potatoes and onions with cooking spray.
Broil until onions and potatoes are tender and brown, about 30 minutes.
Turn potatoes and onions halfway through cooking.

Serves: 4

Nutrition per Serving

Calories	124
Protein	3 grams
Carbohydrate	29 grams
Cholesterol	0 milligrams
Sodium	7 milligrams
Dietary Fiber	3 grams

Exchanges
1 starch
2 vegetable

ROASTED POTATOES WITH RED PEPPERS

EASY - DO AHEAD

ingredients:	2 lbs. potatoes, cut into 1" wedges
	2 large red peppers, diced
	1/2 tsp. salt
	pepper to taste
	cooking spray
directions:	Preheat oven to 400 degrees.
	Spray baking dish with cooking spray.
	Place potatoes and peppers in dish and spray with cooking spray.
	Cook 45 minutes in preheated oven or until potatoes are tender.
	Stir potato-pepper mixture several times during cooking, and spray with cooking spray each time.
	Season with salt and pepper.

Serves: 8

Nutrition per Serving

		Exchanges
Calories	101	1 1/4 starch
Protein	2 grams	
Carbohydrate	24 grams	
Cholesterol	0 milligrams	
Sodium	6 grams	
Dietary Fiber	0 grams	

POTATO FANS

EASY

ingredients:	4 baking potatoes, with skin
	Butter Buds
	1 tbsp. dried parsley
	1 tsp. onion powder
	1/2 tsp. garlic powder
	4 tbsp. fat-free Cheddar cheese, grated
	1 1/2 tbsp. fat-free Parmesan cheese, grated
directions:	Preheat oven to 425 degrees.
	Cut potatoes into thin slices, but do not cut all the way through. The potato slices should "fan" out.
	Place potatoes in a baking dish. Sprinkle generously with Butter Buds, parsley, onion powder, and garlic powder.
	Bake potatoes in preheated oven for 1 hour.
	Remove potatoes from oven and sprinkle with Cheddar and Parmesan cheese.
	Bake potatoes for another 10 to 15 minutes, until they are lightly browned, cheeses are melted and potatoes are soft.

Serves: 4

Nutrition per Serving		**Exchanges**
Calories	168	2 starch
Protein	6 grams	
Carbohydrate	36 grams	
Cholesterol	0 milligrams	
Sodium	95 milligrams	
Dietary Fiber	3 grams	

SPINACH RICE RING
EASY - DO AHEAD

ingredients: 1 cup fat-free rice
1 10 oz. pkg. frozen chopped spinach
1/2 cup finely chopped water chestnuts
5 tsp. lemon juice
1/4 tsp. pepper

directions: Cook the rice according to package directions, without adding butter or salt.

Cook the spinach according to package directions and drain.

Combine the rice, spinach, water chestnuts, lemon juice and pepper.

Spoon the mixture into a 1-quart ring mold lightly sprayed with cooking spray, and pack lightly. Let stand 1 minute and then invert the ring onto a warm serving platter.

Steamed or cooked vegetables (broccoli, cauliflower, carrots, etc...) topped with "Cheese Toast" sauce (see "Brunch" recipe) may be placed in the center of the rice ring.

Serves: 6

Nutrition per Serving
Calories	140
Protein	4 grams
Carbohydrate	30 grams
Cholesterol	0 milligrams
Sodium	61 milligrams
Dietary Fiber	1 gram

Exchanges
1 1/2 starch
1 vegetable

ITALIAN SPAGHETTI SQUASH

AVERAGE

ingredients:
1 large spaghetti squash (about 4 lbs.)
1 large jar fat-free spaghetti sauce (any flavor)
3 carrots, peeled and sliced
2 1/2 cups broccoli florets
1 small zucchini, sliced
1/4 cup grated fat-free Parmesan cheese

directions:
Preheat the oven to 350 degrees.

Pierce the squash in several places and bake for 1 1/4 hours on a baking sheet.

Heat the spaghetti sauce in a saucepan over high heat, bring to a boil, and reduce the heat to medium.

Add the carrots and cook 5 to 6 minutes. Mix in the broccoli, cook for 3 to 5 minutes. Stir in the zucchini and cook for another 2 minutes, or until the vegetables are tender-crisp.

After spaghetti squash has slightly cooled, cut it in half and remove the seeds.

Using a fork, scrape the "spaghetti" onto a platter. Spoon the warm vegetable mixture over the "spaghetti" and sprinkle with fat-free Parmesan cheese.

Serves: 4

Nutrition per Serving		**Exchanges**
Calories	210	1 1/2 starch
Protein	10 grams	4 vegetable
Carbohydrate	43 grams	
Cholesterol	0 milligrams	
Sodium	779 milligrams	
Dietary Fiber	4 grams	

STUFFED TOMATOES

AVERAGE

ingredients:
2 large, firm tomatoes
1/2 cup fat-free sour cream
3 tbsp. chopped green pepper
3 tbsp. sliced green onions
2 tsp. flour
3/4 tsp. sugar
1/4 cup fat-free shredded Monterey Jack cheese
1/4 cup fat-free shredded Cheddar cheese

directions:
Cut the tomatoes in half horizontally, carefully removing seeds and juice of each tomato.
Drain the tomatoes upside-down on paper towels.
Combine the sour cream, peppers, onions, flour, and sugar and mix well.
Place the tomato halves on a foil-lined cookie sheet.
Spoon 1/4 of the sour cream mixture into each tomato cup.
Broil 3 to 5 inches from heat for 2 to 3 minutes, or until sour cream is bubbly and lightly browned.
Sprinkle tomatoes with cheeses and broil 2 to 3 minutes longer, or until cheese is melted.

Nutrition per Serving		Exchanges
Calories	98	1 meat
Protein	11 grams	3 vegetable
Carbohydrate	16 grams	
Cholesterol	0 milligrams	
Sodium	278 milligrams	
Dietary Fiber	1 gram	

ZUCCHINI PANCAKES
EASY - DO AHEAD - FREEZE

ingredients: 4 cups grated zucchini (about 4 medium-size zucchini)
1 cup chopped parsley
1 tsp. lemon pepper
1/2 cup fat-free egg substitute

directions: Combine all ingredients in a large bowl and mix well. Lightly spray a nonstick skillet with cooking spray and heat over medium-high heat until skillet is hot.

Drop zucchini mixture to form 3-inch pancakes and cook until they are golden brown on each side. Spray skillet with cooking spray before cooking each batch of pancakes.

These pancakes can be made ahead of time and frozen.

Serves: 12 to 15 pancakes

Nutrition per Serving		**Exchanges**
Calories	13	1/2 vegetable
Protein	1 gram	
Carbohydrate	1 gram	
Cholesterol	0 milligrams	
Sodium	20 milligrams	
Dietary Fiber	0 grams	

"SAUTEED" ZUCCHINI

EASY - DO AHEAD

ingredients: 6 large zucchini, sliced
3 cloves garlic, chopped
1/4 tsp. red pepper flakes
1 tbsp. balsamic vinegar

directions: Spray a nonstick skillet with cooking spray and heat over medium-high heat. Add zucchini and 1/2 garlic to hot skillet and "saute" about 10 minutes, or until zucchini is softened.
Add remaining garlic and pepper flakes to zucchini mixture and cook 1 to 2 minutes longer.
Remove from heat and cool to room temperature. Sprinkle zucchini mixture with balsamic vinegar and serve.

Serves: 6

Nutrition per Serving

Calories	21
Protein	2 grams
Carbohydrate	4 grams
Cholesterol	0 milligrams
Sodium	4 milligrams
Dietary Fiber	2 grams

Exchanges
1 vegetable

GRILLED VEGETABLE MEDLEY

EASY

ingredients:
2 red potatoes, cut into 1-inch wedges
2 baby eggplants, cut in half lengthwise
2 small zucchini, cut in half lengthwise
1 red pepper, sliced in strips
1 yellow pepper, sliced in strips
1 red onion, cut into wedges
fat-free Italian salad dressing

directions:
Preheat broiler or prepare grill.
Place the potatoes, and enough water to cover, in a saucepan and bring to a boil.
Reduce heat to low, cover and simmer 8 to 10 minutes or until the potatoes are fork-tender. Drain well. Grill the potatoes, eggplant, zucchini, peppers, and onions in batches over medium heat, turning frequently. Brush the vegetables with dressing and grill 5 to 10 minutes or until the vegetables are golden and tender.
Arrange vegetables on a platter and drizzle with dressing.

Serves: 4

Nutrition per Serving

Calories	87
Protein	2 grams
Carbohydrate	20 grams
Cholesterol	0 milligrams
Sodium	62 milligrams
Dietary Fiber	3 grams

Exchanges
1/2 starch
2 vegetable

SPICY VEGETABLES

EASY

ingredients:
1 14 1/2 oz. can fat-free chicken broth
2 carrots, sliced thick
1/2 lb. asparagus, cut in 1" slices
1/4 tbsp. chili powder
1/4 tbsp. ground coriander
1/4 tbsp. ground cumin
1/4 tsp. sugar
1/8 tsp. pepper
1/8 tsp. cinnamon

directions:
In a medium nonstick skillet over high heat, combine the liquid with the carrots and all the seasonings. Bring to a boil, then lower heat and simmer, uncovered, until the carrots are tender-crisp, 6-7 minutes.

Add the asparagus and cook until the vegetables are tender and the liquid is reduced to a glaze, 6-7 minutes longer.

Serves: 4

Nutrition per Serving

Calories	37
Protein	1 gram
Carbohydrate	7 grams
Cholesterol	0 milligrams
Sodium	247 milligrams
Dietary Fiber	1 gram

Exchanges
1 1/2 vegetable

FAT-FREE STUFFING

EASY - DO AHEAD

ingredients:
1 cup minced yellow onion
3/4 cup minced celery
1 cup fat-free chicken broth
2 quarts fat-free croutons for stuffing (Kellogg's Croutettes)
2 tsp. poultry seasoning
1/2 tsp. pepper
1/4 cup parsley, minced
1/2 cup fat-free egg substitute

directions:
Heat 1/2 cup chicken broth over medium-high heat. Add onion and celery to hot broth and cook 5 minutes, or until vegetables are tender.

Mix in croutons, seasonings, egg substitute, and an additional 1/2 chicken broth.

Lightly spray a 2 1/2-quart casserole with cooking spray.

Place stuffing in casserole and bake 1 hour in a 325 degree oven.

Serves: 8

Nutrition per Serving		**Exchanges**
Calories	125	1 1/2 starch
Protein	6 grams	
Carbohydrate	24 grams	
Cholesterol	0 milligrams	
Sodium	452 milligrams	
Dietary Fiber	<1 gram	

ARTICHOKE CASSEROLE
EASY - DO AHEAD

ingredients: 2 - 8 1/2 oz. cans artichoke hearts, drained and quartered
1 bunch scallions, diced (including green)
10 to 12 fat-free saltine crackers, finely crumbled
2 cups fat-free grated Cheddar cheese
3 to 4 dashes Tabasco sauce
pepper to taste
1 1/4 cups fat-free egg substitute

directions: Preheat oven to 350 degrees.
Combine artichokes, scallions, saltines, Cheddar cheese, Tabasco, and pepper in bowl.
Beat egg substitute until frothy.
Fold egg substitute into artichoke mixture and put into baking dish lightly sprayed with cooking spray.
Bake in 350 degree oven for 30 minutes or until hot and bubbly.

Serves: 8

Nutrition per Serving

		Exchanges
Calories	164	2 1/2 meat
Protein	22 grams	1/2 starch
Carbohydrate	16 grams	1 vegetable
Cholesterol	0 milligrams	
Sodium	727 milligrams	
Dietary Fiber	0 grams	

ASPARAGUS DIJON

AVERAGE

ingredients:
2 lbs. asparagus, cooked
1 cup skim milk
2 tbsp. Dijon mustard
1 tbsp. flour
1/4 cup nonfat sour cream
1 tsp. balsamic vinegar
pepper to taste

directions:
Combine the milk, mustard, and flour in a small saucepan and blend well.
Cook over medium heat, stirring occasionally, 3 to 5 minutes or until mixture thickens and is bubbly.
Stir in the sour cream, vinegar, and pepper.
Heat through, and spoon the warm sauce over cooked asparagus.
Serve immediately.

Serves: 8

Nutrition per Serving		Exchanges
Calories	52	2 vegetable
Protein	4 grams	
Carbohydrate	8 grams	
Cholesterol	0 milligrams	
Sodium	113 milligrams	
Dietary Fiber	0 grams	

SWEET AND SOUR BEANS

EASY - DO AHEAD

ingredients: 2 cups pineapple chunks, juice-packed
2 tbsp. vinegar
2 tsp. soy sauce
1 tsp. chicken bouillon granules or 3 tbsp. ketchup
2 tbsp. brown sugar
2 tbsp. cornstarch
2 cups cooked pinto beans, drained
1 green pepper, chopped
1/4 cup mushrooms
1/4 cup peas (optional)
1/4 cup carrots, precooked (optional)
1/2 onion, sliced into rings
3 cups fat-free rice, cooked

directions: Drain pineapple, reserving juice. Add vinegar, soy sauce and bouillon granules or ketchup to juice.
Combine brown sugar and cornstarch.
Add sugar mixture to pineapple juice.
Heat until thickened, stirring constantly.
Remove sauce from heat and add beans, pineapple, green pepper, peas, carrots, mushrooms and onion slices.
Cook over low heat until vegetables are tender.
Serve over rice.

Serves: 6

Nutrition per Serving		Exchanges
Calories	273	1 1/2 starch
Protein	8 grams	2 fruit
Carbohydrate	58 grams	1 vegetable
Cholesterol	0 milligrams	
Sodium	183 milligrams	
Dietary Fiber	1 gram	

Tracy Ann Tallent, Tucson, Arizona

BROCCOLI WITH ORANGE SAUCE

EASY

---

ingredients: 1 1/2 lb. broccoli, cut into spears
6 oz. fat-free cream cheese
1/4 cup skim milk
1/4 tsp. thyme leaves
1/4 cup orange juice

directions: Cook broccoli in boiling water for 10 to 12 minutes or until tender.
Drain broccoli, transfer to a serving dish, and keep warm.
Combine cream cheese, milk, and thyme in a small saucepan and cook over medium heat until smooth.
Add orange juice and mix well.
Pour orange sauce over the broccoli and garnish with orange slices, if desired.

Serves: 6

Nutrition per Serving

Calories	64
Protein	8 grams
Carbohydrate	9 grams
Cholesterol	0 milligrams
Sodium	235 milligrams
Dietary Fiber	0 grams

Exchanges
1 vegetable
1/2 milk

DELECTABLE
DESSERTS

BLACK AND WHITE CHEESECAKE

AVERAGE - DO AHEAD

ingredients:
3/4 cup fat-free granola
16 oz. fat-free cottage cheese
8 oz. fat-free cream cheese
1/4 cup + 1/2 tbsp. flour
1 1/4 cups sugar
4 egg whites
1 tsp. vanilla
2 tbsp. unsweetened cocoa powder
1 tbsp. skim milk

directions:
Preheat oven to 325 degrees.

Place granola in food processor or blender, and blend until slightly ground. Lightly spray 8-inch springform pan with cooking spray and place ground granola in pan.

Combine cottage cheese and cream cheese in food processor or blender, and blend until smooth. Add flour, 1 cup sugar, egg whites, and vanilla to cheese mixture and blend well.

Remove 1/3 cup of cheese mixture from blender; stir in cocoa powder, 1/4 cup sugar, and milk. Pour plain cheese mixture into springform pan. Spoon chocolate mixture over top, swirl into plain batter, but do not blend completely. Bake cheesecake in preheated oven for 50 minutes. Turn oven off and let cake remain in oven for 1 hour, with door slightly open. Remove from oven and allow to cool completely before removing sides of pan.

Serves: 12

Nutrition per Serving		Exchanges
Calories	150	1 1/2 starch
Protein	10 grams	1 meat
Carbohydrate	28 grams	
Cholesterol	5 milligrams	
Sodium	229 milligrams	
Dietary Fiber	< 1 gram	

PINEAPPLE CHEESECAKE

AVERAGE - DO AHEAD

ingredients:
3/4 cup fat-free granola
16 oz. fat-free cottage cheese
8 oz. fat-free cream cheese
1 /4 cup + 2 tbsp. flour
1 1/4 cups sugar
4 egg whites, beaten
1 tsp. vanilla
1 cup crushed pineapple in juice, drained

directions:
Preheat oven to 325 degrees.

Place granola in food processor or blender, and blend until slightly ground. Lightly spray 8-inch springform pan with cooking spray and place ground granola in pan. Combine cottage cheese and cream cheese in food processor or blender, and blend until smooth. Add flour, sugar, egg whites, and vanilla and blend well. Stir pineapple into cheese mixture; then pour into prepared pan. Bake cheesecake in preheated oven for 1 hour.

Turn oven off and let the cake remain in the oven for another hour, with the door slightly open. Remove from oven and allow cake to cool completely before removing sides of pan.

Serves: 12

Nutrition per Servings		**Exchanges**
Calories	158	1 starch
Protein	9 grams	1/2 meat
Carbohydrate	32 grams	1 fruit
Cholesterol	5 milligrams	
Sodium	228 milligrams	
Dietary Fiber	< 1 gram	

LEMON CHEESECAKE WITH BERRY TOPPING

AVERAGE - DO- AHEAD

ingredients:
3/4 cup fat-free granola
16 oz. fat-free cottage cheese
8 oz. fat-free cream cheese
1/4 + 1/2 tbsp. flour
1 1/4 cups sugar
4 egg whites, beaten
1 tbsp. lemon juice
1 tbsp. grated lemon rind
1/4 cup blueberries
1/4 cup strawberries
1/4 cup raspberries

directions:
Preheat oven to 325 degrees.

Place granola in food processor or blender, and blend until slightly ground. Lightly spray 8-inch springform pan with cooking spray and place ground granola in pan.

Combine cottage cheese and cream cheese in food processor or blender, and process until smooth. Add flour, sugar, egg whites, lemon juice, and lemon rind to cheese mixture. Pour into prepared pan and bake in preheated oven for 50 minutes. Turn oven off and let the cheesecake remain in oven for another hour, with the door slightly open. Remove pan from oven and allow cheesecake to cool completely before removing sides of pan. Top cheesecake with mixed berries and serve.

Serves: 12

Nutrition per Serving		Exchanges
Calories	151	2 starch
Protein	9 grams	1/2 meat
Carbohydrate	29 grams	
Cholesterol	5 milligrams	
Sodium	228 milligrams	
Dietary Fiber	< 1 gram	

LIGHT AND LUSCIOUS FROZEN DESSERT

AVERAGE - DO AHEAD - FREEZE

ingredients:

2 lbs. frozen strawberries or blueberries
2 mashed bananas
1 10 oz. package frozen raspberries
1 6 oz. can frozen orange juice
3 tbsp. lemon juice
4 egg whites
1 1/4 cups water
2 cups sugar

directions:

In a large saucepan, boil 3/4 cup water with 2 cups sugar for 5 minutes; then remove from heat.
Add remaining water, frozen fruits, orange juice, and lemon juice and mix well.
Pour into a "freezable" baking dish and freeze until mixture becomes partially frozen.
After first freezing, pour mixture into a bowl and beat thoroughly.
In a separate bowl, beat egg whites until stiff.
Fold egg whites into fruit mixture and freeze.
Beat mixture several times during freezing to make it creamy.

Serves: 12 scoops

Nutrition per Serving		Exchanges
Calories	251	4 fruits
Protein	2 grams	1/4 meat
Carbohydrate	65 grams	
Cholesterol	0 milligrams	
Sodium	21 milligrams	
Dietary Fiber	7 grams	

HONEY-LOUPE FREEZER SORBET

DIFFICULT - DO AHEAD - FREEZE

ingredients:
2 cantaloupes
1 honeydew melon
2 envelopes unflavored gelatin
1 cup light corn syrup
1/4 cup lemon juice

directions:
Remove the peel and seeds from cantaloupes and honeydew melon. Cut fruit into large chunks. Blend cantaloupe chunks in a food processor or blender until smooth.
Pour pureed fruit into 9x9-inch baking dish.
Repeat with honeydew chunks.
In a 1-quart saucepan, evenly sprinkle gelatin over 1/2 cup water and let it stand 1 minute to soften. Cook over medium heat, stirring often, until gelatin dissolves.
Stir 1/2 of gelatin mixture, 1/2 cup corn syrup, and 2 tablespoons lemon juice into each pan of pureed fruit.
Cover each pan and freeze about 3 hours or until partially frozen. Stir several times during freezing.
Spoon cantaloupe mixture into bowl or blender, and blend until fluffy, but still frozen.
Return mixture to baking pan, cover, and freeze until firm, about 2 hours.
Repeat with honeydew mixture.
Before serving, let sorbets stand 10 to 15 minutes at room temperature.

Serves: 8

Nutrition per Serving		Exchanges
Calories	178	3 fruit
Protein	2 grams	
Carbohydrate	44 grams	
Cholesterol	0 milligrams	
Sodium	42 milligrams	
Dietary Fiber	1 gram	

DESSERT PRUNES

EASY

---

ingredients:
12 prunes
6 large or 18 small marshmallows
4 tbsp. granulated or powdered sugar

directions:
In a double boiler, steam prunes for 10 minutes.
Cool and remove pits; then pat dry.
Stuff each prune with 1/2 large marshmallow or 3 small ones.
On wax paper, roll stuffed prunes in sugar.
Super healthy treat!!

Serves: 4 (3 per person)

<u>Nutrition per Serving</u>

Calories	165
Protein	1.2 grams
Carbohydrate	42 grams
Cholesterol	0 milligrams
Sodium	6.6 milligrams
Dietary Fiber	2 grams

<u>Exchanges</u>
3 fruit

MELON MELBA

EASY

ingredients: 1 10 oz. package frozen raspberries in syrup, thawed
2 tbsp. sugar
3 cups honeydew melon cubes or balls
3 cups frozen fat-free vanilla yogurt

directions: Combine the raspberries and sugar in a blender, cover, and blend until smooth.
Strain pureed fruit to remove seeds.
Place 1/2 cup melon cubes in each of 6 dishes and top with 1/2 cup frozen yogurt.
Serve with raspberry sauce.

Serves: 6

Nutrition per Serving		**Exchanges:**
Calories	186	1/2 milk
Protein	5 grams	2 1/3 fruit
Carbohydrate	42 grams	
Cholesterol	0 milligrams	
Sodium	69 milligrams	
Dietary Fiber	3 grams	

FRESH STRAWBERRY-BANANA SORBET

EASY - DO AHEAD - FREEZE

ingredients:
1/3 cup sugar
2/3 cup water
2 tbsp. light corn syrup
1 ripe bananas, cut up
2 cups strawberries

directions:
Combine the sugar, water and corn syrup in a small saucepan and mix well.
Bring mixture to a boil and boil 1 minute.
Cool slightly and refrigerate 30 to 45 minutes or until chilled.
Place banana and strawberries in a food processor or blender, and process until blended.
Gradually add chilled sugar mixture and continue blending until smooth.
Pour mixture into ungreased baking dish, cover and freeze until firm, about 3 to 4 hours.
Stir mixture once during freezing time.

Serves: 6

Nutrition per Serving

Calories	92
Protein	< 1 gram
Carbohydrate	24 grams
Cholesterol	0 milligrams
Sodium	5 milligrams
Dietary Fiber	2 grams

Exchanges:
1 1/2 fruit

RASPBERRY SORBET

DIFFICULT - DO AHEAD - FREEZE

ingredients:
5 1/2 pints fresh raspberries
1 envelope unflavored gelatin
1/3 cup sugar
1 1/4 cups water
3/4 cup light corn syrup
1/4 cup raspberry liqueur
1 tbsp. lemon juice

directions:
Place raspberries in a food processor or blender, and blend until smooth.

Pour the pureed raspberries through a sieve to remove as many seeds as possible.

Sprinkle gelatin over 1 1/4 cups water and let it stand 1 minute to soften.

Cook gelatin over low heat, stirring frequently, until the gelatin is completely dissolved. Stir in the sugar and continue cooking, while continuously stirring, until the sugar dissolves.

Mix raspberries, gelatin mixture, corn syrup, raspberry liqueur, and lemon juice until well blended. Pour the mixture into a 9-inch square pan, cover, and freeze 3 hours, stirring occasionally, until partially frozen.

Transfer the raspberry mixture to a food processor or blender, and blend until smooth but still frozen. Return the mixture to pan, cover, and freeze 2 to 3 hours until firm.

Serves: 8

Nutrition per Serving		Exchanges
Calories	242	4 fruit
Protein	2 grams	
Carbohydrate	56 grams	
Cholesterol	0 milligrams	
Sodium	23 milligrams	
Dietary Fiber	8 grams	

BAKED FRUIT COMPOTE

EASY - DO AHEAD

ingredients: 1 can light cherry pie filling
3/4 cup white wine
1 can mandarin oranges
1 can pineapple chunks and juice
1/2 cup dried prunes
1/2 cup dried apricots

directions: Preheat oven to 350 degrees.
Mix all the ingredients together in a 2-quart casserole lightly sprayed with cooking spray, and bake 45 minutes.

Serves: 8

Nutrition per Serving

Calories	140
Protein	1 gram
Carbohydrate	34 grams
Cholesterol	0 milligrams
Sodium	8 milligrams
Dietary Fiber	2 grams

Exchanges
2 1/4 fruit

FRUIT WITH CARAMEL SAUCE

EASY

ingredients:	1 medium peach, peeled and cut into wedges
	1 kiwi fruit, peeled, sliced
	1 cup strawberries, halved
	1 cup blueberries
	2/3 cup fat-free caramel ice cream topping
	1/4 tsp. rum extract
directions:	Arrange fruit on 6 individual dessert plates.
	In a small saucepan, heat topping and rum extract over medium heat until warm, stirring occasionally.
	Drizzle topping mixture by tablespoon over each serving.

Serves: 6

Nutrition per Serving		**Exchanges**
Calories	125	2 fruit
Protein	1 gram	
Carbohydrate	32 grams	
Cholesterol	0 milligrams	
Sodium	127 milligrams	
Dietary Fiber	2 grams	

FRUITY FROZEN POPS

EASY - DO AHEAD - FREEZE

ingredients:
1 banana, cut in quarters
1 cup crushed pineapple in juice, drained
1 pint strawberries, hulled and sliced
1 cup nonfat vanilla yogurt
1/4 cup honey
8 6 oz. paper cups
8 wooden sticks

directions:
Combine banana, pineapple, strawberries, yogurt and honey in food processor or blender, and blend until very smooth.
Fill paper cups with fruit mixture, place a wooden stick in the center of each, and freeze.

Serves: 8

Nutrition per Serving

Calories	101
Protein	2 grams
Carbohydrate	25 grams
Cholesterol	0 milligrams
Sodium	21 milligrams
Dietary Fiber	1 gram

Exchanges
1 1/4 fruit
1/4 milk

YOGURT MELON-RING SUPREME

EASY

---

ingredients: 4 slices cantaloupe, cut into rings
3/4 cup fresh strawberries, chopped
2 kiwi fruit, peeled, chopped
1 tbsp. honey
2 cups lemon or pineapple fat-free frozen yogurt

directions: Place cantaloupe rings on individual plates.
In a small bowl, combine strawberries, kiwi fruit, and honey and toss lightly.
Place 1/2 cup yogurt in center of each melon ring and spoon strawberry mixture over yogurt and melon.

Serves: 4

Nutrition per Serving
Calories	152
Protein	5 grams
Carbohydrate	40 grams
Cholesterol	0 milligrams
Sodium	66 milligrams
Dietary Fiber	2.3 grams

Exchanges
1/2 milk
2 fruit

PINEAPPLE SANDWICHES
AVERAGE - DO AHEAD

ingredients:
4 tbsp. brown sugar
1/3 cup chopped dates
1/4 cup fat-free cream cheese
2 tsp. orange juice
8 slices fresh pineapple, with core

directions:
Combine dates and 2 tablespoons sugar in food processor or blender, and blend until finely chopped. Add cream cheese and blend, scraping sides. Preheat broiler and lightly spray a broiler tray with cooking spray.

Stir 2 tablespoons brown sugar and orange juice in a small dish. Cut a 1-inch "X" in the center of each pineapple slice.

Spoon the date-cheese mixture on 4 slices, dividing equally. Spread evenly over the slices, leaving a 1/4-inch border.

Top with remaining pineapple slices, pressing together. Brush the top of each sandwich with the sugar/orange mixture.

Place sandwiches 3 inches from heat, for 5 minutes per side, or until lightly browned and filling is hot. Brush with the brown sugar mixture after turning over.

Let sandwiches stand 10 minutes before serving. The date/cheese filling can be made 4 days ahead and kept refrigerated.

Serves: 4

Nutrition per Serving

Calories	150	
Protein	2 grams	
Carbohydrate	5 milligrams	
Cholesterol	2 milligrams	
Sodium	105 milligrams	
Dietary Fiber	2 grams	

Exchanges
2 fruit
1/2 meat

FRUIT DELIGHT

EASY - DO AHEAD

ingredients: 2 peaches
2 pears
1 can pineapple chunks
3 bananas
Strawberries
Lemon juice

directions: Cut peaches and pears into large bite-size pieces. Cut bananas into 1-inch slices.
Baste peaches, pears, and bananas with lemon juice.
Place fruit, alternately, on plastic colored tooth-picks.

Serves: 5

Nutrition per Serving

Calories	152
Protein	0 grams
Carbohydrate	38 grams
Cholesterol	0 milligrams
Sodium	0 milligrams
Dietary Fiber	1 gram

Exchanges:
2 1/2 fruit

BERRY DELIGHT

EASY - DO AHEAD

ingredients:	3/4 cup strawberries, cut in half
	3/4 cup blueberries
	1/2 cup raspberries
	1/2 cup fat-free sour cream
	2 tbsp. brown sugar
directions:	Combine blueberries, strawberries, and raspberries in a glass bowl.
	Combine sour cream and brown sugar and blend well.
	Top berries with cream-sugar mixture and serve.

Serves: 4

Nutrition per Serving

Calories	68
Protein	3 grams
Carbohydrate	15 grams
Cholesterol	0 milligrams
Sodium	110 milligrams
Dietary Fiber	3 grams

Exchanges
1 fruit
1/2 meat

APPLE CRISP
EASY - DO AHEAD

ingredients: 4 cups canned apple pie filling
1 tbsp. lemon juice
1/2 cup flour
3/4 cup brown sugar
3/4 cup multi-grain oatmeal
1 tsp. cinnamon
1/4 tsp. nutmeg
1 tbsp. low-fat butter

directions: Preheat oven to 375 degrees.
Lightly spray a 2-quart baking dish with nonfat cooking spray.
Place apple slices in dish and sprinkle with lemon juice.
In a small bowl, combine flour, brown sugar, oatmeal, cinnamon and nutmeg.
Using a fork or pastry blender, cut butter into mixture and mix until crumbly but slightly moist.
Sprinkle over apples.
Bake in preheated oven for 15 minutes.
Reduce temperature to 350 degrees and bake for an additional 20 minutes.

Serves: 4

Nutrition per Serving

Calories	169
Protein	1 gram
Carbohydrate	40 grams
Cholesterol	0 milligrams
Sodium	47 milligrams
Dietary Fiber	< 1 gram

Exchanges:
1/2 starch
2 fruit

APPLE HONEY CAKE
EASY - DO AHEAD - FREEZE

---

ingredients:
2 cups honey
3/4 cup fat-free egg substitute
1 1/3 cups sugar
2 cups chunky natural applesauce
4 cups flour
1 tsp. baking soda
1 tsp. ground cinnamon
1 tsp. ginger

directions:
Preheat oven to 350 degrees.
Combine honey and egg substitute in a large bowl.
Add sugar, applesauce, flour, baking soda, cinnamon, and ginger.
Lightly spray 2 loaf pans with cooking spray and divide honey cake batter between the two pans.
Bake in a preheated oven for 50 minutes, or until toothpick comes out clean when inserted in center of cake.

Yields: 2 loaf cakes (12 to 14 slices)

Nutrition per Serving
Calories	185
Protein	3 grams
Carbohydrate	44 grams
Cholesterol	0 milligrams
Sodium	49 grams
Dietary Fiber	< 1 gram

Exchanges
1 starch
1 3/4 fruit

HEAVENLY ANGEL FOOD CAKE

AVERAGE - DO AHEAD

ingredients:

1 1/4 cups powdered sugar
1 cup flour
1 2/3 cups egg whites (12 to 14)
1 1/2 tsp. cream of tartar
2 tsp. vanilla
1 1/4 cups sugar
1 tsp. grated orange peel

directions:

Preheat oven to 375 degrees.

Combine powdered sugar and flour; set aside. In a large bowl, with mixer at high speed, beat egg whites and cream of tartar until stiff peaks form. Beat in vanilla extract. Continue beating at high speed, sprinkling in sugar 2 tablespoons at a time. Beat until sugar is completely dissolved. Fold in flour mixture and orange peel until flour disappears.

Pour batter into ungreased 10-inch tube pan.

Bake 30 to 35 minutes, until cake springs back when lightly touched.

Invert cake in pan on glass bottle, and cool completely in pan. Carefully loosen cake with knife or long spatula and place in plate.

Great with fresh fruit!!

Serves: 12

Nutrition per Serving		Exchanges
Calories	172	1 3/4 starch
Protein	5 grams	1/2 fruit
Carbohydrate	39 grams	
Cholesterol	0 milligrams	
Sodium	55 milligrams	
Dietary Fiber	0 grams	

STRAWBERRY-ORANGE SHORTCAKE

EASY

---

ingredients: 2 8 oz. containers nonfat vanilla yogurt
2 tbsp. frozen orange juice concentrate, thawed
2 cups sliced fresh strawberries
1 10 oz. package frozen raspberries, thawed
1 package fat-free pound cake, cut into 8 slices

directions: Combine the yogurt and orange juice in a mixing bowl and blend well.
In a separate bowl, combine strawberries and raspberries and mix lightly.
To serve, place cake slices on individual dessert plates.
Spoon 1/3 cup fruit mixture over each slice and top each with 3 tablespoons yogurt mixture.

Serves: 8

Nutrition per Serving

Calories	269
Protein	7 grams
Carbohydrate	60 grams
Cholesterol	1 milligram
Sodium	275 milligrams
Dietary Fiber	2 grams

Exchanges

1 starch
2 1/2 fruit
1/2 milk

ANGEL FOOD CAKE TRIFLE

EASY - DO AHEAD

ingredients:
1 angel food cake (best if day-old)
2 small boxes sugar-free Jell-O (any flavor)
Lite Cool Whip

directions:
Break cake into pieces and place in glass bowl.
Prepare Jell-O according to package directions, but do not refrigerate to gel.
Pour liquid Jell-O mixture on top of cake.
Push cake down until it absorbs the Jell-O.
Place mixture in refrigerator until Jell-O sets.
Top cake with Lite Cool Whip before serving.

Serves: 8

Nutrition per Serving
Calories	159
Protein	5 grams
Carbohydrate	33 grams
Cholesterol	0 milligrams
Sodium	205 milligrams
Dietary Fiber	0 grams

(Cool Whip not included)

Exchanges
2 starch

CHERRY VANILLA CUSTARD CAKE

EASY - DO AHEAD

ingredients: 1 prepared angel food cake
2 packages instant vanilla pudding
3 cups cold skim milk
2 cups fat-free sour cream
1 can cherry, strawberry or blueberry pie filling

directions: Tear cake into small pieces and put in a 9x13-inch pan.
In a bowl, mix milk, sour cream, and pudding until thickened. Spread over cake.
Let chill for 30 minutes.
Spread pie filling on top of cake. Chill.
Can be made a day ahead.

Serves: 8

Nutrition per Serving

		Exchanges
Calories	392	3 starch
Protein	12 grams	2 1/2 fruit
Carbohydrate	81 grams	
Cholesterol	6 milligrams	
Sodium	583 milligrams	
Dietary Fiber	0 grams	

FRUIT YOGURT FROZEN SALAD

EASY - DO AHEAD - FREEZE

ingredients:
1 cup sugar
1 cup fat-free sour cream
2 8 oz. cartons fat-free flavored or vanilla yogurt
1 16 oz. can chunky mixed fruit, drained

directions:
Combine the sugar, sour cream and yogurt in a large bowl and mix well.
Pour mixture into a 9-inch square pan, cover, and freeze until firm (about 5 to 6 hours or overnight).
Allow frozen salad to stand at room temperature for 10 to 15 minutes before serving.

Serves: 8

Nutrition per Serving
Calories	154
Protein	4 grams
Carbohydrate	34 grams
Cholesterol	0 milligrams
Sodium	43 milligrams
Dietary Fiber	0 grams

Exchanges
1/2 milk
2 fruit

TRIFLE FRUIT SALAD
EASY - DO AHEAD

ingredients:
2 cups fresh pineapple chunks
2 cups strawberries, sliced
1 pint blueberries
2 cups seedless green grapes
1 1/4 cups skim milk
1/2 cup fat-free sour cream
1 3 3/4 oz. package instant banana cream pudding and pie filling mix
1 8 oz. can crushed pineapple, undrained

directions:
In a large glass bowl, layer the fruits.
Combine the milk and sour cream and blend well.
Add the pudding mix and beat until well blended, about 2 minutes.
Stir in the crushed pineapple.
Spoon the pudding mixture over the fruit to within 1 inch of the edges.
Cover and refrigerate several hours.

Serves: 12

Nutrition per Serving

Calories	82
Protein	2 grams
Carbohydrate	19 grams
Cholesterol	0 milligrams
Sodium	57 milligrams
Dietary Fiber	1 gram

Exchanges
1 fruit
1/4 milk

PLUM CREME
AVERAGE - DO AHEAD

ingredients:
4 plums, pitted, sliced
2 oz. fat-free cream cheese
2 tbsp. sugar
1 cup nonfat vanilla yogurt
2 tsp. unflavored gelatin
2 tbsp. water

directions:
Combine plums, cream cheese, and sugar in blender or food processor, and blend until smooth, about 1 minute.

Add yogurt to plum mixture.

Combine gelatin and water in a small saucepan and cook over low heat until dissolved.

While the blender or food processor is running, add the hot gelatin to the plum mixture and continue blending until it is thoroughly mixed, about 10 seconds.

Spoon mixture into individual dessert dishes and refrigerate, at least 30 minutes.

Keep stored in refrigerator.

Serves: 8

Nutrition per Serving

Calories	61
Protein	3 grams
Carbohydrate	12 grams
Cholesterol	0 milligrams
Sodium	69 milligrams
Dietary Fiber	1 gram

Exchanges
1/2 fruit
1/4 milk

PEACH-BANANA BREAD PUDDING

EASY - DO AHEAD

---

ingredients: 8 slices fat-free bread, cut into 1-inch cubes (about 3 1/2 cups)
1 1/2 cups evaporated skimmed milk
4 egg whites, lightly beaten
1/2 cup frozen apple juice concentrate (defrosted)
1 16 oz. can juice-packed peaches, drained and chopped
2 ripe bananas, sliced
1 tsp. lemon juice
1 1/4 tsp. cinnamon
1/4 tsp. ground nutmeg
1/3 cup maple syrup (low-calorie, optional)
1 tsp. vanilla

directions: Preheat oven to 325 degrees.
In a large bowl, combine the bread cubes, evaporated milk, egg whites, apple juice concentrate, peaches, bananas, lemon juice, cinnamon, nutmeg, maple syrup, and vanilla, and mix well.
Pour mixture into 8x11-inch baking dish lightly sprayed with cooking spray. Bake 60 to 65 minutes at 325 degrees, or until toothpick inserted in center comes out clean.
Cool slightly. Can be served warm or cold.

Serves: 8

Nutrition per Serving		**Exchanges**
Calories	199	1 starch
Protein	8 grams	1/2 milk
Carbohydrate	33 grams	1 fruit
Cholesterol	2 milligrams	
Sodium	199 milligrams	
Dietary Fiber	3 grams	

QUICK PUDDING PARFAITS

EASY - DO AHEAD

ingredients:
1 cup skim milk
8 oz. nonfat lemon yogurt
1/4 to 1/2 tsp. grated lemon peel
1 small package instant vanilla pudding
2 to 3 cups fresh fruit

directions:
Combine milk, yogurt, lemon peel and pudding mix in a small bowl.
Beat pudding mixture 2 minutes at low speed or until mixture has slightly thickened.
In 6 parfait glasses, make two alternate layers beginning with fruit.
Chill until serving time.
Garnish with sliced fruit.

Serves: 6

Nutrition per Serving

Calories	125
Protein	3 grams
Carbohydrate	28 grams
Cholesterol	1 milligram
Sodium	142 milligrams
Dietary Fiber	1 gram

Exchanges
1/2 milk
1/2 starch
1/2 fruit

Deena Goodale, Glendale, Arizona

RICE PUDDING

EASY - DO AHEAD

ingredients:
1/2 cup fat-free rice
2 cups skim milk
1/2 cup raisins
3/4 cup sugar
1 1/2 cups fat-free egg substitute
2 tbsp. vanilla extract
cinnamon to taste

directions:
Combine rice and milk in a large saucepan and bring to a boil.

Lower heat and simmer, uncovered, 30 to 40 minutes, stirring occasionally.

Add raisins to rice mixture and simmer 5 minutes longer.

Add sugar and stir into rice until completely dissolved.

Mix egg substitute and vanilla together in a bowl, and beat well.

Fold egg mixture into rice and stir over low heat until it is completely blended and thickened.

Pour rice pudding into serving dish and sprinkle cinnamon on top.

Can be served warm or cold.

Serves: 8

Nutrition per Serving		Exchanges
Calories	285	1/2 milk
Protein	15 grams	1 starch
Carbohydrate	55 grams	2 fruit
Cholesterol	6 milligrams	1 meat
Sodium	255 milligrams	
Dietary Fiber	< 1 gram	

APPLE PUDDING

AVERAGE - DO AHEAD

ingredients:
1 cup matzo farfel
1 cup boiling water
3/4 cup fat-free egg substitute
4 tart apples, peeled, cored, and grated
1/2 cup raisins
1 1/4 cups sugar
3 tbsp. lemon juice
1 tbsp. lemon rind
2 tbsp. sweet wine
4 tbsp. honey
3/4 tsp. cinnamon

directions:
Preheat oven to 350 degrees.

Combine matzo farfel and boiling water in a large bowl. Set aside to cool.

Add beaten egg substitute to farfel.

Combine grated apples and raisins in a separate bowl and slowly fold in farfel mixture. Add cinnamon and sugar. Lightly spay a 1 1/2-quart baking dish with cooking spray and heat in oven for 3 minutes.

Pour farfel mixture into baking dish and bake 25 minutes.

Place lemon juice, lemon rind, wine, and honey in a saucepan and bring to a boil.

Pour over farfel pudding and bake an additional 25 minutes or until the top is golden brown.

Serves: 6

Nutrition per Serving		**Exchanges**
Calories	395	4 fruit
Protein	6 grams	2 starch
Carbohydrate	95 grams	
Cholesterol	0 milligrams	
Sodium	54 milligrams	
Dietary Fiber	3 grams	

CHOCOLATE MERINGUES
DIFFICULT

MERINGUES

ingredients:
 2 large egg whites
1/4 tsp. cream of tartar
1 1/3 cups sugar

directions: In a small bowl, beat egg whites and cream of tartar with mixer at high speed. Gradually sprinkle in sugar, beating well after each addition, until sugar dissolves and whites stand in stiff peaks. Preheat oven to 200 degrees. Line cookie sheet with foil; spoon 4 meringues into 4-inch round shape. Shape each round to form a nest. Bake 2 1/2 to 3 hours, until crisp, but not brown. Cool cookies, then remove from foil.

FILLING

ingredients:
1 tsp. unflavored gelatin
1/4 cup evaporated skim milk, well chilled
2 tbsp. sugar
1 tbsp. cocoa

directions: In small saucepan, sprinkle gelatin over 2 tablespoons cold water. Let it stand 1 minute so gelatin slightly softens. Cook over low heat until gelatin completely dissolves, stirring occasionally. Cool slightly. In small bowl, beat chilled evaporated skim milk, with mixer at high speed, until stiff peaks form. Immediately spoon 1/4 of the filling mixture into each cooled meringue shell.

Serves: 4

Nutrition per Serving		Exchanges:
Calories	301	2 starch
Protein	6 grams	2 1/2 fruit
Carbohydrate	71 grams	
Cholesterol	.6 milligram	
Sodium	50 milligrams	
Dietary Fiber	0 grams	

FAT-FREE FABULOUS CARAMEL APPLES

EASY - DO AHEAD

---

ingredients:
8 apples (your favorite kind)
16 tbsp. fat-free caramel topping
Wax paper
Wooden sticks

directions:
Using your favorite apples, insert a wooden stick into each apple.
Warm caramel topping in microwave (30 seconds to 1 minute) or on stove top (place jar of caramel in a pot of boiling water for 3 to 5 minutes).
Dip apples in caramel.
Place on wax paper to harden a little.
Indulge and love every minute of it!!
Sliced apples can be individually dipped in the caramel topping, if desired.

Nutrition per Serving		Exchanges
Calories	211	3 1/2 fruit
Protein	1 gram	
Carbohydrate	51 grams	
Cholesterol	0 milligrams	
Sodium	71 milligrams	
Dietary Fiber	3 grams	

Lori L. Feldman, Gilbert, Arizona

DESIRABLE
DRINKS

BLUEBERRY BANANA SHAKE

EASY

---

ingredients: 1 pint nonfat vanilla frozen yogurt
1 cup skim milk
1 cup blueberries
1 ripe banana

directions: Place all ingredients in a blender, and blend at high speed until smooth.

Serves: 4

Nutrition per Serving

Calories	158
Protein	6 grams
Carbohydrate	33 grams
Cholesterol	1 milligram
Sodium	98 milligrams
Dietary Fiber	1 gram

Exchanges
1 milk
2 fruit

BANANA SHAKE

EASY - DO AHEAD

ingredients: 1 ripe banana
1/4 cup skim milk
1 tbsp. nonfat chocolate syrup or hot fudge
5 ice cubes
1/2 tbsp. sugar (optional)

directions: Combine all the ingredients, except ice cubes, in a covered blender. Blend 30 seconds.
Add ice cubes, two at a time.
Cover and blend.
Repeat until ice cubes are gone, and process until smooth.
If too thick, add additional milk.

Serves: 1

Nutrition per Serving

Calories	204
Protein	4 grams
Carbohydrate	50 grams
Cholesterol	1 milligram
Sodium	63 milligrams
Dietary Fiber	2 grams

Exchanges
1/4 milk
3 fruit

STRAWBERRY SHAKE

EASY

ingredients: 10 to 12 frozen unsweetened strawberries
1/2 cup skim milk
1/4 cup nonfat vanilla yogurt
1 tsp. sugar

directions: Combine all ingredients in a blender, and blend on high until smooth.

Serves: 1

Nutrition per Serving		Exchanges
Calories	154	1 milk
Protein	7 grams	1 fruit
Carbohydrate	31 grams	
Cholesterol	3 milligrams	
Sodium	101 milligrams	
Dietary Fiber	3 grams	

RASPBERRY MINT TEA

EASY - DO AHEAD

ingredients:
3 bags mint-flavored herbal tea
2 cups frozen unsweetened raspberries, thawed
1/3 cup sugar
3 tbsp. lemon juice
1 cup ice cubes

directions:
In a medium-size saucepan, bring 5 cups water to a boil.
Place tea bags in a medium heat-proof bowl.
When water boils, pour over tea bags and steep 5 minutes.
Remove tea bags and discard.
Cover tea and refrigerate at least 30 minutes.
Blend raspberries in blender until smooth.
Strain raspberry puree to discard seeds. Blend chilled tea, raspberry puree, sugar, lemon juice, and ice cubes. Blend mixture until smooth.

Serves: 6

Nutrition per Serving

Calories	63
Protein	0 grams
Carbohydrate	16 grams
Cholesterol	0 milligrams
Sodium	1 milligram
Dietary Fiber	1 gram

Exchanges
1 fruit

RASPBERRY-PEACH ICED TEA

EASY - DO AHEAD

ingredients: 1/2 pint raspberries
1 medium-size ripe peach, peeled and thinly sliced
2 tea bags

directions: Place raspberries, peach slices, and tea bags in a 2-quart pitcher.
Pour 1 1/2 quarts boiling water over fruit and tea bags.
Chill tea for several hours. Remove tea bags.
Pour over ice cubes and serve.

Serves: 6

Nutrition per Recipe   **Exchanges**
Calories   16   1/4 fruit
Protein   < 1 gram
Carbohydrate   4 grams
Cholesterol   0 milligrams
Sodium   0 milligrams
Dietary Fiber   1 gram

QUICK PEACH PAPAYA FIZZ

EASY

---

ingredients:
1 16 oz. can sliced peaches in syrup, drained
1 papaya, peeled and cut in chunks
5 tbsp. sugar
2 tbsp + 2 tsp. grenadine syrup
1 1/2 tsp. grated lime zest
4 tsp. lime juice
2 cups crushed ice
4 1/2 cups plain seltzer

directions:
Combine peaches, papaya, sugar, grenadine, lime zest, and lime juice in a blender.
Blend until smooth, and refrigerate fruit mixture until ready to serve.
Add about 6 tablespoons fruit mixture, then stir in 1/4 cup seltzer until well blended.
To serve, spoon 1/3 cup crushed ice into each glass.
Top each drink with another 1/2 cup seltzer.

Serves: 6

Nutrition per Serving

Calories	103
Protein	0 grams
Carbohydrate	27 grams
Cholesterol	0 milligrams
Sodium	11 milligrams
Dietary Fiber	1 gram

Exchanges
1 1/2 fruit

PINEAPPLE-TANGERINE REFRESHER

EASY

ingredients: 3 tangerines
1/2 pineapple, sliced
1 32 oz. bottle sodium-free seltzer, chilled
2 tbsp. sugar (optional)

directions: Squeeze the juice from the tangerines into a small bowl.
Chop pineapple slices in a food processor or blender until coarsely chopped.
Place pineapple and juice in a 2-quart pitcher and add tangerine juice.
Stir in seltzer and sugar. Pour over ice.

Serves: 6

Nutrition per Serving		**Exchanges**
Calories	58	1 fruit
Protein	0 grams	
Carbohydrate	15 grams	
Cholesterol	0 milligrams	
Sodium	0 milligrams	
Dietary Fiber	1 gram	

MICROWAVE
MAGIC

HOT CRAB DIP

EASY

ingredients: 8 oz. fat-free cream cheese
8 oz. fat-free crabmeat or crab flakes
2 tbsp. skim milk
1 tbsp. minced onion
1 tbsp. lemon juice
1 tsp. cream-style horseradish

directions: Place cream cheese in a 1-quart casserole and microwave on MEDIUM for 1 1/2 to 2 minutes, just to soften.
Stir in crabmeat, milk, onion, lemon juice, and horseradish.
Cover with plastic wrap, vented, and microwave for 3 to 5 minutes until heated through.

Yields: 2 cups
Serves: 6

Nutrition per Serving		Exchanges
Calories	65	1 meat
Protein	9 grams	1/2 starch
Carbohydrate	7 grams	
Cholesterol	6 milligrams	
Sodium	5 milligrams	
Dietary Fiber	0 grams	

CHEESY CRAB CRISPS

EASY - DO AHEAD

ingredients: 8 oz. fat-free crabmeat or crab flakes
1 1/2 tbsp. green onion, sliced
1 1/4 cup fat-free Swiss cheese, shredded
1/2 cup fat-free mayonnaise
1 tsp. lemon juice
1/4 tsp. garlic puree
36 fat-free crackers

directions: Combine flaked crabmeat, onion, cheese, mayonnaise, lemon juice, and garlic puree.
Place one spoonful of crab mixture on each cracker and arrange in a circle on a microwave-safe dish. Cook on HIGH 1 minute for every 12 appetizers, until thoroughly heated.
Turn dish halfway through cooking time.

Yields: 3 dozen
Serves: 8 (4 to 5 per person)

Nutrition per Serving		Exchanges
Calories	131	1 starch
Protein	8 grams	1 meat
Carbohydrate	15 grams	
Cholesterol	2 milligrams	
Sodium	617 milligrams	
Dietary Fiber	0 grams	

CRUNCHY-MUNCHY VEGETABLE ROUNDS

EASY

---

ingredients:
1/4 cup diced green onions
3 tbsp. chopped fresh mushrooms
3 tbsp. shredded carrot
2 tsp. fat-free Italian salad dressing
1 large cucumber, cut into rounds
1/4 cup shredded fat-free mozzarella cheese

directions:
Combine green onions, mushrooms, carrots and salad dressings in a microwave-safe bowl and cook on HIGH 2 minutes.

Top each cucumber slice with green onion mixture and sprinkle with mozzarella cheese.

Place vegetable rounds in a circle on a microwave dish, reduce heat to MEDIUM, and cook 1 to 2 minutes or until cheese is melted.

Serves: 6

Nutrition per Serving

Calories	26
Protein	3 grams
Carbohydrate	2 grams
Cholesterol	0 milligrams
Sodium	76 milligrams
Dietary Fiber	1 gram

Exchanges
1 vegetable

QUESADILLAS

EASY

ingredients:
1 cup fat-free shredded Cheddar cheese
1 cup fat-free shredded mozzarella cheese
1 4 oz. can diced green chilies, drained
1 1/2 medium tomatoes, chopped
8 6-inch fat-free corn tortillas
salsa (optional)
fat-free sour cream (optional)

directions:
Combine cheeses in a bowl.
Place 1 tortilla on a microwave-safe dish and sprinkle with 1/4 cup cheese.
Top with 1 tablespoon green chilies and tomatoes.
Microwave quesadilla on MEDIUM 1 minute or until cheese is melted.
Garnish with salsa and sour cream, if desired.
Fold tortilla in half and repeat with remaining tortillas.

Serves: 8

Nutrition per Serving

Calories	142
Protein	16 grams
Carbohydrate	15 grams
Cholesterol	0 milligrams
Sodium	498 milligrams
Dietary Fiber	2 grams

Exchanges
1 starch
2 meat

CHILI QUESO BEAN DIP
EASY - DO AHEAD

ingredients:
1 16 oz. can fat-free refried beans
2 cups fat-free shredded Cheddar cheese
1/2 cup mild chunky salsa
1 7 oz. can diced green chilies, drained
1/4 tsp. garlic puree
1/2 tsp. onion powder
Tabasco sauce, to taste

directions:
Combine all the ingredients in a microwave-safe bowl.
Stir well and cover with vented plastic wrap.
Cook on HIGH 5 to 7 minutes until cheese is melted and dip is thoroughly heated.
Stir dip halfway through cooking.

Yields: 2 1/2 cups
Serves: 6

Nutrition per Serving
Calories	163
Protein	17 grams
Carbohydrate	21 grams
Cholesterol	0 milligrams
Sodium	1070 milligrams
Dietary Fiber	3 grams

Exchanges
1 starch
1 meat
1 vegetable

EGGPLANT YOGURT DIP

AVERAGE - DO AHEAD

ingredients:
1 lb. eggplant
1 onion, minced
1/2 green bell pepper, diced
1 tsp. garlic puree
1 tsp. lemon juice
pepper to taste
1 cup plain nonfat yogurt

directions:
Pierce eggplant with a fork and microwave on HIGH 6 to 7 minutes, until soft. Let eggplant cool.
Combine onion, green pepper, garlic and lemon juice in a bowl.
Cook on HIGH 1 1/2 to 2 minutes, or until vegetables are soft.
Cut eggplant open and scoop out the center.
Add eggplant to onion-pepper mixture and blend well. Add pepper and stir in yogurt until well blended.
Cover and refrigerate dip until well chilled.
Great with toasted pita chips!!

Yields: 2 cups
Serves: 6

Nutrition per Serving		Exchanges
Calories	52	1 vegetable
Protein	3 grams	1/4 milk
Carbohydrate	10 grams	
Cholesterol	< 1 milligram	
Sodium	32 milligrams	
Dietary Fiber	2 grams	

SPINACH DIP, IN LOAF
AVERAGE - DO AHEAD

ingredients: 2 packages (10 oz. each) frozen chopped spinach
8 oz. fat-free cream cheese
1 cup fat-free sour cream
1/2 cup fat-free mayonnaise
1/4 cup finely-chopped green onion
1 tsp. seasoned salt substitute
Fat-free round or loaf sourdough bread or crackers

directions: Microwave spinach according to package directions. Drain well and set aside.

Microwave cream cheese in a 2-quart microwave-safe bowl for 1 1/2 minutes on MEDIUM to soften.

Mix in the sour cream, mayonnaise, onion, seasoned salt, and drained spinach.

If using bread, scoop out center of loaf, leaving 2 inches on the bottom.

Before serving, spoon spinach-cheese filling into the loaf and microwave on MEDIUM 1 1/2 to 2 minutes, or until the bread is warm.

Serve with bread cubes, fat-free crackers, or assorted fresh vegetables.

Serves: 16

Nutrition per Serving*

Calories	30
Protein	3 grams
Carbohydrate	3 grams
Cholesterol	0 milligrams
Sodium	139 milligrams
Dietary Fiber	1 gram

Exchanges
1/4 starch
1/2 vegetable

*Nutritional analysis does not include bread or crackers.

SHRIMP DIP

EASY

---

ingredients:
8 oz. fat-free cream cheese
1 7 oz. can shrimp, cut up, drained
2 tsp. ketchup
1 tsp. instant minced onion
1 tsp. prepared mustard
1 tsp. Worcestershire sauce
1/4 tsp. garlic powder

directions:
Place cream cheese in a 1-quart casserole and microwave on MEDIUM for 1 1/2 to 2 minutes, just to soften.

Stir in shrimp, ketchup, onion, mustard, Worcestershire sauce, and garlic powder.

Cover with plastic wrap, vented, and microwave on MEDIUM for 3 to 5 minutes, or until heated through.

Yields: 2 cups
Serves: 6

Nutrition per Serving

		Exchanges
Calories	64	1 meat
Protein	11 grams	1/3 starch
Carbohydrate	4 grams	
Cholesterol	55 milligrams	
Sodium	366 milligrams	
Dietary Fiber	0 grams	

FRENCH TOAST

EASY

---

ingredients: 1 cup fat-free egg substitute, beaten
8 tsp. skim milk
1/2 tsp. vanilla
4 slices fat-free white or whole-wheat bread
1/4 tsp. cinnamon

directions: Combine egg, milk, and vanilla in a bowl.
Dip each bread slice in mixture and coat well.
Let bread soak 1 minute and place on microwave-safe plate.
Cook on MEDIUM 1 minute.
Turn bread slice over and cook 1 minute more, or until center is set.
Sprinkle with cinnamon and serve with low-calorie syrup, powdered sugar or low-calorie jelly.

Serves: 2

<u>**Nutrition per Serving**</u>

Calories	141	
Protein	15 grams	
Carbohydrate	21 grams	
Cholesterol	0 milligrams	
Sodium	371 milligrams	
Dietary Fiber	4 grams	

<u>**Exchanges**</u>
1 1/2 starch
1 meat

HUEVOS RANCHEROS
EASY

---

ingredients: 4 6-inch fat-free corn tortillas
1/2 cup fat-free refried beans
2 cups fat-free egg substitute
1/2 cup skim milk
3/4 cup shredded fat-free Monterey Jack cheese
6 to 8 tsp. diced green chilies
pepper to taste
1/2 cup fat-free salsa

directions: Wrap each tortilla in a paper towel and cook on HIGH 1 minute, to soften.
Transfer to a plate and repeat with remaining tortillas.
Spread 2 tablespoons refried beans on each tortilla and cook a few seconds to heat.
Combine eggs, milk, cheese, chilies and pepper in a small bowl, and cook on HIGH 2 to 3 minutes.
Stir several times during cooking, pushing the undercooked egg from the center to the edge.
Continue cooking eggs until they are barely set.
Spread 1/4 egg mixture over each tortilla and top with salsa.

Serves: 4

Nutrition per Serving

Calories	241	
Protein	29 grams	
Carbohydrate	25 grams	
Cholesterol	1 milligram	
Sodium	846 milligrams	
Dietary Fiber	2.7 grams	

Exchanges
1 1/2 starch
3 meat
1 vegetable

CREAMY SCRAMBLED EGGS

EASY

---

ingredients: 1 cup fat-free egg substitute, beaten
3 oz. fat-free cream cheese
1/4 cup skim milk
1/2 red or yellow bell pepper, diced
1/4 tsp. garlic powder
pepper to taste

directions: Combine all ingredients in a 1 1/2-quart micro-wave-safe dish, and cook on MEDIUM 5 to 7 minutes, stirring often during cooking.
(Eggs will still look wet when they are done.)
Let stand 1 minute, to set, before serving.

Serves: 4

Nutrition per Serving

Calories	56	
Protein	10 grams	
Carbohydrate	4 grams	
Cholesterol	0 milligrams	
Sodium	258 milligrams	
Dietary Fiber	0 grams	

Exchanges
1 meat
1/3 milk

VERY VEGGIE OMELET

EASY

ingredients:
3/4 cup fat-free egg substitute
1/2 tsp. garlic powder
pepper to taste
1/2 cup chopped onion
1/2 cup sliced fresh mushrooms
1/4 cup diced yellow pepper
1/4 cup diced red pepper
1 1/2 cups fat-free shredded mozzarella cheese

directions:
Combine onion, mushrooms, and peppers in a microwave-safe dish. Cover tightly with plastic wrap, and cook on HIGH 2 minutes, or until vegetables are slightly soft.
Drain vegetables well.
Beat egg substitute with garlic powder and pepper in a mixing bowl, and stir in cheese.
Pour egg mixture over cooked vegetables and cook on MEDIUM 8 to 10 minutes or until eggs are set. Turn dish halfway through cooking time.

Serves: 6

Nutrition per Serving

Calories	115
Protein	22 grams
Carbohydrate	2 grams
Cholesterol	0 milligrams
Sodium	456 milligrams
Dietary Fiber	0 grams

Exchanges
3 meat
1/2 vegetable

HOT AND HEALTHY
BREAKFAST CEREAL

EASY - DO AHEAD

---

ingredients: 1 cup instant nonfat dry milk powder
1/2 cup oat bran
2/3 cup quick-cooking oats
1/3 cup raisins
1/3 cup chopped dates
1 1/2 tsp. cinnamon

directions: Combine the milk powder, oat bran, oats, raisins, dates and cinnamon in a large bowl.
Combine 1/3 cup cereal mixture with 2/3 cup water in a microwave-safe bowl and cook on HIGH 2 to 3 minutes, stirring every minute during cooking.
Let stand 2 minutes before serving.

Serves: 8

Nutrition per Serving

		Exchanges
Calories	110	1 starch
Protein	5 grams	1/2 fruit
Carbohydrate	23 grams	
Cholesterol	2 milligrams	
Sodium	48 milligrams	
Dietary Fiber	2 grams	

FRUITY BIALY SNACKS

EASY - DO AHEAD

ingredients: 3 oz. fat-free cream cheese
1 tbsp. thawed frozen orange juice concentrate
1 tbsp. grated orange peel
4 tsp. Grape-Nuts or fat-free granola
4 bialys, cut in half and toasted
2 cups fresh berries (strawberries, blueberries, raspberries, etc.)

directions: Microwave cream cheese in a bowl on MEDIUM, 1 minute or until softened.
Blend in orange peel, orange juice concentrate and cereal.
Spread each toasted bialy half with 1/8 cheese mixture and top with 1/4 cup berries.

Serves: 8

Nutrition per Serving		Exchanges
Calories	67	1/2 fruit
Protein	3 grams	1/2 starch
Carbohydrate	12 grams	
Cholesterol	0 milligrams	
Sodium	127 milligrams	
Dietary Fiber	1 gram	

HOT POTATO SOUP

AVERAGE - DO AHEAD

ingredients:
5 cups fat-free chicken broth
3 cups skim milk
4 large baking potatoes, peeled and cut into chunks
2 onions, cut in chunks
2 carrots, peeled and cut in chunks
2 celery stalks, cut in chunks
salt substitute and pepper to taste

directions:
Place cut-up vegetables with chicken broth in a large casserole, cover, and microwave on HIGH 15 to 20 minutes, or until all vegetables are tender. Keep the vegetable mixture covered.
Place 1/4 of the vegetable mixture at a time in a blender or food processor, and puree until smooth. Place pureed mixture in a large bowl and repeat process with remaining vegetables.
Stir milk into pureed vegetable mixture and cook, uncovered, on HIGH 8 to 10 minutes, or until hot. Season with salt substitute and pepper.

Serves: 4

Nutrition per Serving

Calories	244
Protein	16 grams
Carbohydrate	45 grams
Cholesterol	3 milligrams
Sodium	827 milligrams
Dietary Fiber	5 grams

Exchanges
1 milk
1 1/2 starch
1 vegetable

CREAM OF BROCCOLI SOUP

EASY - DO AHEAD

ingredients: 2 10 oz. packages frozen chopped broccoli
2 cups skim milk
1 1/2 cups fat-free chicken broth
2 tsp. onion powder
3 tbsp. flour
salt substitute and pepper to taste

directions: Cook broccoli according to package directions until tender, but not soft. Drain well.

Combine half the broccoli, milk, chicken broth, onion powder, and flour in a blender or food processor, and blend.

Add the remaining broccoli, milk and broth, and blend well.

Pour soup into a large microwave-safe bowl, cover with plastic wrap, and cook on MEDIUM 8 to 10 minutes, until thickened.

Stir soup every 3 to 4 minutes during cooking.

Season with salt substitute and pepper.

Serves: 4

Nutrition per Serving

		Exchanges
Calories	101	1/2 milk
Protein	8 grams	2 vegetable
Carbohydrate	17 grams	
Cholesterol	2 milligrams	
Sodium	428 milligrams	
Dietary Fiber	4 grams	

SWEET AND SOUR SAUCE

EASY - DO AHEAD

ingredients: 2 tbsp. cornstarch
1/2 cup sugar
1/4 cup cold water
1 15 1/2 oz. can crushed pineapple (in its own juice)
1/2 cup chopped green pepper
3/4 tsp. garlic powder
2 tbsp. low-sodium soy sauce
1/2 cup cider vinegar
8-10 drops Tabasco sauce

directions: Stir sugar, cornstarch, and water together in a microwave-safe dish.
Stir in pineapple, green pepper, garlic powder, soy sauce, vinegar, and Tabasco sauce, and mix well.
Microwave on HIGH 5 to 7 minutes, or until mixture becomes thickened.
Stir sauce several times during cooking.
Allow sauce to stand 5 to 10 minutes before serving.

Yields: 1 1/2 to 2 cups
Serves: 8

Nutrition per Serving

		Exchanges
Calories	67	1 fruit
Protein	< 1 gram	
Carbohydrate	18 grams	
Cholesterol	0 milligrams	
Sodium	154 milligrams	
Dietary Fiber	< 1 gram	

CRANBERRY SAUCE

EASY - DO AHEAD

ingredients: 6 cups fresh cranberries
2/3 cup fresh orange juice
2 cups sugar

directions: Combine all ingredients in a microwave-safe bowl
and cover with vented plastic wrap.
Cook on HIGH 6 to 7 minutes until the cranberries
begin to pop open.
Stir sauce, cover, and refrigerate several hours
before serving.

Yields: 4 cups
Serves: 8

Nutrition per Serving

Calories	238	**Exchanges**	
Protein	< 1 gram	4 fruit	
Carbohydrate	61 grams		
Cholesterol	0 milligrams		
Sodium	1 milligram		
Dietary Fiber	3 grams		

TOMATO PASTA SAUCE

EASY - DO AHEAD

ingredients: 32 oz. low-sodium tomato sauce
12 oz. low-sodium tomato paste
2/3 cup fat-free beef broth
2 tbsp. brown sugar
2 tsp. Worcestershire sauce
1 tsp. oregano
1 1/2 tsp. minced garlic
1 tsp. basil
pepper to taste

directions: Combine tomato sauce, tomato paste, beef broth, brown sugar, Worcestershire sauce, and seasonings in a microwave-safe dish and cover with vented plastic wrap.
Microwave on HIGH 12 to 14 minutes until very hot. Stir tomato sauce halfway through cooking time.

Serves: 8

Nutrition per Serving

Calories	83
Protein	4 grams
Carbohydrate	19 grams
Cholesterol	0 milligrams
Sodium	872 milligrams
Dietary Fiber	3.5 grams

Exchanges
3 vegetable

SIMPLY DIVINE SOLE

AVERAGE

ingredients:
8.3 oz. sole fillets
3/4 cup dry white wine
1/2 cup water
2 tbsp. dried parsley
2 green onions, thinly sliced
1/8 tsp. pepper
2 tsp. cornstarch
1 lemon, thinly sliced

directions:
Combine wine, 1/4 cup water, parsley, onions, and pepper in a small bowl and set aside. Place fillets in a single layer in a microwave-safe dish, with thickest parts toward the outside of the dish. Top the fillets with lemon slices and pour the wine mixture on top.

Cover with plastic wrap; microwave on HIGH 3 minutes.

Move the outside pieces toward the center of the dish and continue cooking on HIGH 1 to 2 minutes longer, or until fish turns opaque and flakes easily in the thickest part.

Remove fish and lemon slices and pour the liquid into a glass bowl. Dissolve the cornstarch in the remaining 1/4 cup water and stir into the hot liquid from fish. Microwave on HIGH 2 to 3 minutes, until the mixture becomes slightly thickened, stirring several times during cooking.

Pour sauce over fish and serve immediately.

Serves: 8

Nutrition per Serving		**Exchanges**
Calories	90	2 meat
Protein	14 grams	1/2 vegetable
Carbohydrate	2 grams	
Cholesterol	90 milligrams	
Sodium	64 milligrams	
Dietary Fiber	< 1	

"FRIED" FILLETS
EASY

---

ingredients: 4 3 oz. flounder fillets
1 tbsp. fat-free mayonnaise
3 tbsp. fat-free sour cream
1 tsp. cornstarch
1/2 tsp. mustard
1/2 tsp. dried tarragon
1/3 cup cornflake crumbs
garlic powder, onion powder, pepper to taste

directions: Combine cornstarch and sour cream in a small bowl and blend well. Stir mayonnaise, mustard, and tarragon into sour cream mixture.

Spread mayonnaise mixture on fillets to coat well. Combine cornflake crumbs and other seasonings in a separate bowl and coat fillets with crumb mixture.

Place fillets in a single layer in a microwave- safe dish, with the thickest portions toward the outside of the dish. Microwave fillets on HIGH 2 minutes. Rearrange fish, moving outside pieces to the center of the dish.

Continue cooking on HIGH 2 to 3 minutes or until fish turns opaque and begins to flake easily in the thickest part. Let fish stand 3 minutes before serving.

Serves: 4

Nutrition per Serving
Calories	109
Protein	16 grams
Carbohydrate	7 grams
Cholesterol	40 milligrams
Sodium	184 milligrams
Dietary Fiber	0 grams

Exchanges
2 meat
1/2 starch

SWEET-AND-SOUR FISH FILLETS

EASY

ingredients:
1 lb. haddock fillets
2 tsp. low-sodium teriyaki sauce
1 8 oz. can crushed pineapple (packed in its own juice), drained
1 green bell pepper, cut in thin strips
1 tomato, cut into 6 wedges

directions:
Place fish fillets in a single layer in a microwave-safe baking dish, with the thickest parts of the fish toward the outside of the dish.
Coat fish with teriyaki sauce and top with drained pineapple, green pepper slices, and tomato wedges. Cover with waxed paper, and cook on HIGH 3 minutes.
Move outside fillets toward center of dish and continue cooking on HIGH, 1 to 2 minutes longer, or until fish turns opaque and flakes in the thickest part.

Serves: 4

Nutrition per Serving

Calories	146
Protein	22 grams
Carbohydrate	12 grams
Cholesterol	65 milligrams
Sodium	180 milligrams
Dietary Fiber	1 gram

Exchanges
3 meat
1 1/2 vegetable

SPINACH-STUFFED SOLE

AVERAGE - DO AHEAD

ingredients:
3 oz. sole fillets
1 10 oz. package frozen chopped spinach
3/4 cup fat-free sour cream
1 tbsp. cornstarch
1/2 cup chopped green onions
1 1/2 tsp. lemon juice
1/2 tsp. garlic powder

directions:
Cook spinach in microwave oven according to package directions. Drain well.

Combine the spinach, sour cream, cornstarch, green onions, lemon juice, and garlic powder in a microwave-safe bowl, and microwave on HIGH 1 1/2 to 2 minutes.

Spread equal portions of spinach mixture down the center of each sole fillet and roll, securing the fillet with a wooden toothpick.

Place fish rolls in a 9x11-inch baking dish and microwave on HIGH 3 minutes.

Move outside rolls to center of dish and continue cooking on HIGH 2 to 3 minutes longer, or until fish turns opaque and flakes in center.

Serves: 6

Nutrition per Serving		Exchanges
Calories	107	2 1/2 meat
Protein	18 grams	1/2 vegetable
Carbohydrate	4 grams	
Cholesterol	40 milligrams	
Sodium	119 milligrams	
Dietary Fiber	1 gram	

"FRIED" FISH

EASY

ingredients: 1 lb. haddock, cut in chunks
1/2 cup fat-free Italian dressing
1/3 cup cracker crumbs, fat-free
garlic powder to taste
onion powder to taste
1/3 cup fat-free Parmesan cheese

directions: Pour Italian dressing into a small bowl.
Combine cracker crumbs, garlic powder, onion powder, and Parmesan cheese in a separate bowl.
Dip each fish chunk in salad dressing, then roll in crumb mixture to coat well.
Place fish in a circle on a microwave-safe dish, and cook on HIGH 2 minutes.
Move outside fish pieces in center of dish and continue cooking on HIGH 1 to 2 minutes, or until fish flakes in center.

Serves: 4

Nutrition per Serving		**Exchanges**
Calories	159	3 meat
Protein	24	1/2 starch
Carbohydrate	10 grams	
Cholesterol	65 milligrams	
Sodium	290 milligrams	
Dietary Fiber	< 1 gram	

FISH KABOBS
EASY - DO AHEAD

ingredients:
1 green bell pepper, cut into 12 pieces
2 onions, cut into 6 wedges
12 whole mushrooms
12 whole cherry tomatoes
1 lb. haddock, cut in thick chunks
1 cup low-sodium teriyaki sauce

directions:
Combine the bell pepper pieces, onion wedges, mushrooms, tomatoes, and fish pieces in a bowl. Pour teriyaki sauce over vegetable-fish mixture, cover, and refrigerate for several hours.

Using 6 wooden skewer, place two pepper pieces, two mushrooms, two tomatoes, one onion wedge, and several pieces of fish on each skewer.

Arrange kabobs in a 9x13-inch microwave-safe baking dish. Cover baking dish with waxed paper and cook on MEDIUM 8 minutes.

Move outside skewers to center of dish, baste with marinade, and continue to cook on MEDIUM 8 minutes.

Move outside skewers to center of dish, baste with marinade, and continue to cook on MEDIUM 8 minutes or until fish is cooked and bell pepper is tender.

Serves: 6

Nutrition per Serving
Calories	129
Protein	18 grams
Carbohydrate	13 grams
Cholesterol	43 milligrams
Sodium	1658 milligrams
Dietary Fiber	2 grams

Exchanges
1 1/2 meat
2 1/2 vegetable

HAPPY HOUR CRAB COCKTAIL

EASY - DO AHEAD

ingredients: 1 lb. fat-free Crab Delights
1/2 cup ketchup
1 to 2 tbsp. prepared horseradish
2 tbsp. lemon juice
1 tsp. Worcestershire sauce
Tabasco sauce to taste

directions: Combine the ketchup, horseradish, lemon juice, Worcestershire sauce, and Tabasco sauce in a small bowl and mix well.
Serve the crab with the dipping sauce.

Serves: 4 to 6

Nutrition per Serving
Calories	134	
Protein	11 grams	
Carbohydrate	21 grams	
Cholesterol	12 milligrams	
Sodium	996 milligrams	
Dietary Fiber	0 grams	

Exchanges
1 meat
1 1/4 starch

CREOLE FISH WITH RICE

AVERAGE

ingredients: 16 oz. fish fillets (haddock), cut in 6 portions
1 - 15 1/2 oz. can low-sodium tomato sauce
1 cup chopped green bell pepper
1 cup sliced fresh mushrooms
1 cup chopped onion
1 cup fat-free rice
2 1/2 cups water
salt and pepper to taste

directions: Combine 2 1/2 cups water and brown rice in a microwave-safe bowl. Cover with plastic wrap and vent at corner. Microwave rice on HIGH 5 to 6 minutes, until bubbly.

Reduce heat to MEDIUM and continue cooking 25 to 30 minutes or until liquid is absorbed.

Set rice aside and keep warm.

Place fish fillets in a microwave-safe baking dish, with the thickest parts toward the outside of the dish.

Combine tomato sauce, bell pepper, mushrooms, and onion and spoon over fish. Microwave 7 to 9 minutes on HIGH, or until fish flakes easily with a fork at thickest portion. Rearrange fillets after 3 minutes of cooking time, moving center pieces toward outside.

Serve fish over rice.

Serves: 6

Nutrition per Serving

Calories	206
Protein	18 grams
Carbohydrate	30 grams
Cholesterol	43 milligrams
Sodium	85 milligrams
Dietary Fiber	1 gram

Exchanges
2 meat
2 vegetable
1 starch

SEAFOOD RICE CASSEROLE

EASY

ingredients:
1 cup Crab Delights
3/4 cup uncooked fat-free rice
1 3/4 cups water
3/4 tsp. onion powder
1 cup fat-free sour milk
1/2 cup skim milk
pepper to taste
1/2 cup fat-free shredded Cheddar cheese

directions: Combine rice and water in a microwave-safe dish, cover, and cook on HIGH 10 minutes.

Stir rice, cover, and microwave an additional 10 minutes.

Add onion powder, sour cream, milk, pepper, and cooked crab to rice and stir well.

Microwave rice mixture on HIGH 10 to 12 minutes, rotating and stirring halfway through cooking time. Sprinkle cheese over top of casserole and cook 1 minute, or until cheese is melted.

Serves: 4

Nutrition per Serving

		Exchanges
Calories	240	1 milk
Protein	16 grams	1 meat
Carbohydrate	35 grams	1 1/4 starch
Cholesterol	5 milligrams	
Sodium	448 milligrams	
Dietary Fiber	0 grams	

TERIYAKI VEGETABLES WITH RICE

EASY - DO AHEAD

ingredients:	1 16 oz. package frozen broccoli, cauliflower, and carrot medley
	1 cup low-sodium teriyaki sauce
	1 can sliced water chestnuts, drained
	1 can bamboo shoots, drained
	4 cups fat-free cooked rice
directions:	Place frozen vegetables in a microwave-safe 9x11-inch baking dish.
	Coat vegetables with 1/2 cup teriyaki sauce.
	Cover with vented plastic wrap and cook according to package directions (but do not add water).
	Mix cooked vegetables with cooked rice, water chestnuts, and bamboo shoots.
	Pour 3/4 to 1 cup teriyaki sauce over vegetable mixture and mix well.
	Cover casserole and microwave 5 minutes longer on HIGH heat, until well heated.

Serves: 4

Nutrition per Serving

Calories	198	
Protein	8 grams	
Carbohydrate	43 grams	
Cholesterol	0 milligrams	
Sodium	1062 milligrams	
Dietary Fiber	4.8 grams	

Exchanges
2 starch
2 vegetable

CHEESY MANICOTTI
EASY - DO AHEAD - FREEZE

ingredients:
1 5 oz. package manicotti shells
1 8 oz. package fat-free cream cheese
1 cup fat-free ricotta cheese
1 cup fat-free shredded mozzarella cheese
1/2 cup fat-free egg substitute
2 tbsp. chopped fresh parsley
1/8 tsp. pepper
2 1/2 cups fat-free spaghetti sauce
1/2 cup fat-free Parmesan cheese

directions:
Cook manicotti shells according to package directions and drain well. Blend the cream cheese until smooth and mix with the ricotta cheese. Stir the mozzarella cheese, egg substitute, parsley, and pepper into the cheese mixture. Fill each manicotti shell with 1/4 cup cheese filling.
Pour 1 1/4 cups spaghetti sauce over the bottom of a microwave-safe baking dish.
Place manicotti filled shells on top of sauce and pour remaining sauce over the shells.
Cover with vented plastic wrap and cook on medium heat 20 minutes, or until hot and bubbly.
Sprinkle Parmesan cheese on top and cook an additional 1 to 2 minutes, until cheese is melted.

Serves: 6

Nutrition per Serving

Calories	270
Protein	31 grams
Carbohydrate	31 grams
Cholesterol	6.6 milligrams
Sodium	971 milligrams
Dietary Fiber	0 grams

Exchanges
2 starch
3 meat

CREAMY NOODLE CASSEROLE

EASY - DO AHEAD

ingredients:
1 12 oz. package egg-free noodles
1 cup fat-free cottage cheese
1 cup fat-free sour cream
1 tsp. onion powder
1/2 tsp. Worcestershire sauce
2 to 3 drops Tabasco sauce
1 cup fat-free shredded Cheddar cheese

directions:
Cook noodles according to package directions and place in a microwave-safe casserole.

Add cottage cheese, sour cream, onion powder, Worcestershire sauce, and Tabasco sauce to noodles and mix well.

Cover casserole and microwave on HIGH 8 to 10 minutes or until very hot.

Stir noodle mixture halfway through cooking time.

Serves: 8

Nutrition per Serving

Calories	204
Protein	14 grams
Carbohydrate	35 grams
Cholesterol	0 milligrams
Sodium	116 milligrams
Dietary Fiber	0 grams

Exchanges
2 starch
1 meat

AU GRATIN POTATOES

EASY - DO AHEAD

ingredients: 3 baking potatoes, thinly sliced
1/2 onion, chopped
1/3 cup water
1/2 cup skim milk
1 tsp. dried chives
3/4 cup fat-free shredded Cheddar cheese

directions: Combine sliced potatoes, onion, and water in a microwave-safe dish.
Cover with vented plastic wrap and cook on HIGH 9 to 10 minutes, or until tender-crisp.
Stir potatoes halfway through cooking time.
Stir milk, chives, and 1/2 cup cheese into potato mixture.
Sprinkle top with remaining 1/4 cup cheese and cook, uncovered, on MEDIUM 3 to 4 minutes, or until cheese is melted.

Serves: 6

Nutrition per Serving

		Exchanges
Calories	107	1/3 milk
Protein	6 grams	1 starch
Carbohydrate	19 grams	
Cholesterol	0 milligrams	
Sodium	155 milligrams	
Dietary Fiber	2 grams	

CHEESY CAULIFLOWER

EASY

ingredients: 1 large head cauliflower
2 tbsp. fat-free mayonnaise
1/2 tsp. prepared mustard
1/2 cup fat-free shredded Cheddar cheese

directions: Remove the stem and leaves from cauliflower, rinse under cold water, and leave damp.
Place whole cauliflower in a microwave-safe dish and cover with vented plastic wrap.
Microwave on HIGH 8 to 9 minutes, or until tender.
Combine mayonnaise with mustard and spoon over top of cauliflower.
Sprinkle Cheddar cheese on top and return to microwave for 45 seconds to 1 minute, or until cheese is melted.

Serves: 4

Nutrition per Serving

Calories	46
Protein	6 grams
Carbohydrate	6 grams
Cholesterol	0 milligrams
Sodium	212 milligrams
Dietary Fiber	2 grams

Exchanges
1 vegetable
1/2 meat

MARINATED VEGGIES

EASY - DO AHEAD

ingredients: 1 15 oz. can salt-free tomato sauce
1/2 cup water
3/4 cup thinly sliced celery
1 tsp. garlic powder
1/4 tsp. dried dill
1/2 tsp. dried oregano
1/4 tsp. dried tarragon
3/4 cup fresh cauliflower florets
1 cup fresh broccoli florets
1 cup sliced carrots

directions: Combine the tomato sauce, water, celery, garlic powder, dill, oregano, and tarragon in a micro-wave-safe dish and cover with vented plastic wrap.
Microwave on HIGH 6 minutes, or until boiling.
Stir in cauliflower, broccoli, and carrots.
Cover baking dish, reduce heat to MEDIUM, and cook 4 to 6 minutes or until vegetables are tender-crisp.
Stir mixture several times during cooking.
Serve hot or cold.

Serves: 8

<ins>Nutrition per Serving</ins>		<ins>Exchanges</ins>
Calories	40	2 vegetable
Protein	2 grams	
Carbohydrate	8 grams	
Cholesterol	0 milligrams	
Sodium	34 milligrams	
Dietary Fiber	2 grams	

RATATOUILLE

EASY - DO AHEAD

ingredients:
2 tomatoes, chopped
2 zucchini, sliced thin
1 eggplant, peeled and cubed
1 onion, sliced thin
1/2 green bell pepper, sliced into strips
1 tsp. minced garlic
1/2 tsp. dried basil
1/2 tsp. dried oregano
1 tbsp. fat-free Parmesan cheese

directions:
Place all the ingredients in a microwave-safe baking dish and cover with plastic wrap.
Microwave on HIGH for 8 to 10 minutes, or until the vegetables are tender.
Stir vegetables every 3 minutes during cooking.
Serve hot or cold.

Serves: 6

Nutrition per Serving

Calories	48
Protein	2 grams
Carbohydrate	11 grams
Cholesterol	0 milligrams
Sodium	15 milligrams
Dietary Fiber	4 grams

Exchanges
2 vegetable

HOLIDAY FRUIT COMPOTE

EASY - DO AHEAD

ingredients:
1 lb. can sliced peaches, drained
1 12 oz. package dried apricots
1 16 oz. can pitted bing cherries
3/4 cup brown sugar
1/2 cup orange juice
1/4 cup lemon juice

directions:
Drain juice from bing cherries into a small bowl.
Add brown sugar, orange juice, and lemon juice to cherry juice and mix well.
Combine the peaches, apricots, and drained cherries in a microwave-safe dish.
Pour sugar-juice mixture over fruit, cover with plastic wrap, and cook on HIGH 14 to 16 minutes.
Allow compote to cool, then refrigerate overnight before serving.

Serves: 8

Nutrition per Serving

Calories	178
Protein	2 grams
Carbohydrate	46 grams
Cholesterol	0 milligrams
Sodium	11 milligrams
Dietary Fiber	1 gram

Exchanges
3 fruit

PUMPKIN PUDDING

EASY - DO AHEAD

---

ingredients:

1/2 cup fat-free egg substitute
1 cup canned pumpkin
1/3 cup brown sugar
1/2 tsp. pumpkin pie spice
1 12 oz. can evaporated skim milk
fat-free granola (optional)

directions:

Combine egg substitute, pumpkin, brown sugar, and pumpkin spice in a microwave-safe bowl.
Stir in milk and cook on HIGH 5 to 6 minutes or until mixture becomes thick,
Stir pudding and turn dish several times during cooking.
Reduce heat to MEDIUM and continue cooking 7 to 9 minutes or until toothpick inserted into center of pudding comes out clean, when tested.
Sprinkle granola over top of pudding, if desired.

Serves: 6

Nutrition per Serving*

Calories	120
Protein	7 grams
Carbohydrate	23 grams
Cholesterol	3 milligrams
Sodium	112 milligrams
Dietary Fiber	1 gram

Exchanges

1/2 milk
1 starch

*Nutritional analysis does not include granola.

POLYNESIAN BREAD PUDDING

EASY

---

ingredients:
3 slices fat-free bread, cubed
1 8 oz. can crushed pineapple, drained
1/4 cup raisins
1/2 cup skim milk
1/2 cup fat-free egg substitute
1 tsp. vanilla extract
1 tsp. cinnamon
2 tbsp. brown sugar

directions:
Combine bread cubes with raisins and drained pineapple in a microwave-safe dish.

In a separate bowl, beat the egg substitute, milk and vanilla.

Mix brown sugar and cinnamon together in a small cup.

Pour egg mixture over bread and sprinkle sugar-cinnamon on top.

Cook on MEDIUM 10 to 12 minutes or until toothpick inserted into the center comes out clean when tested.

Serves: 6

Nutrition per Serving

Calories	97	
Protein	4 grams	
Carbohydrate	17 grams	
Cholesterol	0 milligrams	
Sodium	96 milligrams	
Dietary Fiber	2 grams	

Exchanges
1 1/4 starch

STRAWBERRY MOUSSE

EASY - DO AHEAD

ingredients:
1 envelope unflavored gelatin
2/3 cup cold water
2 cups fat-free strawberry-flavored yogurt
1/2 cup chopped strawberries
2 tsp. sugar

directions:
Place 1/3 cup water in a bowl and sprinkle gelatin over the water.

Let the gelatin stand 1 minute and stir until blended.

Microwave 40 to 60 seconds on HIGH or until gelatin is dissolved, stirring once.

Stir in the other 1/3 cup cold water.

Blend yogurt with gelatin mixture until very smooth.

Stir in chopped strawberries and sugar.

Divide mousse among 4 glasses and refrigerate at least 1 hour before serving.

Serves: 4

Nutrition per Serving

Calories	64
Protein	6 grams
Carbohydrate	10 grams
Cholesterol	3 milligrams
Sodium	72 milligrams
Dietary Fiber	0 grams

Exchanges
3/4 milk

CHOCOLATE PUDDING

EASY - DO AHEAD

---

ingredients:
1 tbsp. unsweetened cocoa powder
1 1/2 tbsp. sugar
1 1/3 tbsp. cornstarch
1 cup skim milk
1/2 tsp. chocolate extract
1/2 tsp. vanilla

directions:
Combine cocoa, sugar, and cornstarch in a 1-quart microwave-safe bowl.
Add milk and mix well.
Microwave, uncovered, on HIGH for 2 minutes and stir well. Continue cooking 1 to 2 minutes longer until mixture thickens.
Stir in chocolate flavoring and vanilla.
Cool slightly before serving.
Cover and refrigerate until ready to serve.

Serves: 2

Nutrition per Serving

Calories	121
Protein	5 grams
Carbohydrate	26 grams
Cholesterol	2 milligrams
Sodium	72 milligrams
Dietary Fiber	0 grams

Exchanges
1/2 milk
1 1/3 fruit

BAKED APPLES

EASY

---

ingredients:
4 small apples, rinsed and cored
4 tsp. raisins
2 tsp. ground cinnamon
4 tsp. brown sugar
1/2 cup apple juice

directions:
Peel skin from the apples and place in a microwave-safe baking dish.

Fill the center of each apple with 1 teaspoon raisins.

Combine the cinnamon and sugar and sprinkle 1 1/2 teaspoons over raisins.

Pour 2 tablespoons apple juice over each apple.

Cover apples with waxed paper and cook on HIGH 2 to 3 minutes per apple.

Let apples stand several minutes before serving.

Serves: 4

Nutrition per Serving		Exchanges
Calories	130	2 fruit
Protein	0 grams	
Carbohydrate	34 grams	
Cholesterol	0 milligrams	
Sodium	4 milligrams	
Dietary Fiber	3 grams	

CRUSTLESS PUMPKIN PIE

EASY - DO AHEAD

ingredients:
16 oz. canned pumpkin
1/2 cup evaporated skim milk
1/2 cup sugar
3 large egg whites, lightly beaten
2 tsp. ground pumpkin pie spice
1 tbsp. flour

directions:
Combine all the ingredients in a microwave-safe dish and beat until smooth.

Microwave, uncovered, for 5 minutes on HIGH, stirring often.

Turn microwave to MEDIUM and cook an additional 12 to 15 minutes, or until the center is almost set.

Let pumpkin "pie" stand 10 minutes to set.

Serves: 6

<u>**Nutrition per Serving**</u>

Calories	119
Protein	5 grams
Carbohydrate	27 grams
Cholesterol	< 1 milligram
Sodium	27 milligrams
Dietary Fiber	2 grams

<u>**Exchanges**</u>
1 1/2 starch

HAPPY HOLIDAY
MENUS

NEW YEAR'S BRUNCH

Mimosas or Quick Peach Papaya Fizz* - page 236
Crustless Spinach Quiche* or - page 54
Vegetable Frittata* - page 52
Assorted Bialys
Fat-free Cream Cheese
Assorted Jellies
Fruited Cottage Cheese* - page 100
Assorted Fat-free Muffins
Coffee

VALENTINE'S DAY

Chilled Strawberry Soup* - page 34
Happy Hour Shrimp Cocktail* - page 264
Spinach Stuffed Sole* - page 261
Au Gratin Potatoes* - page 179
Strawberry Mousse* - page 277

PASSOVER DINNER

Fat-free Chicken Broth with Matzo Balls* - page 36
Delectable Fish Fillets* - page 141
Carrot Tzimmis* - page 162
Broccoli with Orange Sauce* - page 198
Apple Pudding* - page 227

EASTER DINNER

Artichoke Pita Chips* - page 26
Hot Spinach Salad* - page 77
Creole Fish with Rice* - page 265
Asparagus Dijon* - page 196
Trifle Fruit Salad* - page 222

FOURTH OF JULY PICNIC

Raw Vegetables with Spinach Dip* - page 5
Honey Mustard Potato Salad* - page 79
Sweet Pepper Slaw* - page 93
Teriyaki Vegetable Kabobs
Fat-free Garlic Bread* - page 49
Apple Crisp* - page 215
Raspberry Peach Iced Tea* - page 235

THANKSGIVING DINNER

Onion Cheese Puffs* - page 24
Crunchy Munchy Vegetable Rounds* - page 241
Simply Divine Sole* - page 258
Fat-free Stuffing* - page 194
Pineapple Sweet Potatoes* - page 171
Tangy Green Beans* - page 166
Cranberry Sauce* - page 256
Crustless Pumpkin Pie - page 280

HANNUKAH DINNER

Chicken-flavored Vegetable Soup* with - page 37
Fat-free Matzo Balls* - page 36
Orange Jello Mold* - page 90
Sweet and Sour Fish Fillets* - page 260
Potato Kugel* or - page 173
Zucchini Pancakes* - page 190
Applesauce
Fresh Steamed Vegetable Medley with
Cheese Sauce* (Cheese Toast recipe) - page 67
Apple Honey Cake* - page 216
Fresh Cut-up Fruit

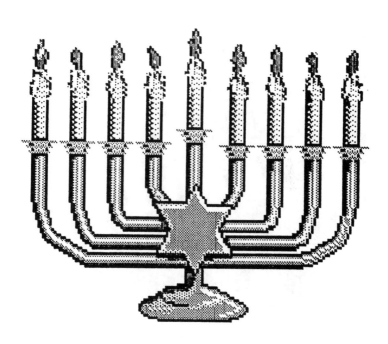

CHRISTMAS DINNER

Artichoke Dip* - page 4
Fat-free Crackers or Assorted Fresh Vegetables
Outrageous Caesar Salad* - page 83
Vegetarian Lasagna* - page 151
Fat-free Sourdough or Garlic Bread* - page 49
Pumpkin Pudding* or - page 275
Holiday Fruit Compote - page 274*

LUNCHEON

Raspberry Mint Tea* - page 234
Artichoke Dip* - page 4
Fat-free Crackers
Crab and Vegetable Salad* - page 71
Fat-free Sourdough Bread
Heavenly Angel Food Cake - page 217*
Fresh Fruit

ITALIAN DINNER

Stuffed Mushrooms* - page 25
Minestrone Soup* - page 35
Cheesy Manicotti* - page 268
Fat-free Garlic Bread* - page 49
Fat-free Frozen Yogurt
Chocolate Meringues* - page 228

MEXICAN FIESTA

BRUNCH OR LUNCHEON

Hot and Spicy Tomato Salsa* - page 14
Quesadillas* - page 242
Chili Relleno Casserole* - page 57
Mexican Rice* - page 158
Fruit and Cabbage Slaw* - page 95
Melon Melba* - page 205

DINNER

Mexican Layer Dip* - page 12
Fat-free Tortilla Chips
Mexican Chili Bean Coleslaw* - page 97
Vegetable Burrito Casserole* - page 117
Cheese Enchiladas* - page 114
Light and Luscious Frozen Dessert* - page 202

FAT FREE LIVING 1

15202 North 50th Place • Scottsdale, Arizona 85254 • (602) 996-6300

Please send me _____ copies of your cookbook at $14.95 each plus $4.00 for postage , sales tax, and handling. Enclosed is my check payable to FAT FREE LIVING for $_____.

Name _____

Address _____

City _____ State _____ Zip _____

— —

FAT FREE LIVING 2

15202 North 50th Place • Scottsdale, Arizona 85254 • (602) 996-6300

Please send me _____ copies of your cookbook at $15.95 each plus $4.00 for postage , sales tax, and handling. Enclosed is my check payable to FAT FREE LIVING for $_____.

Name _____

Address _____

City _____ State _____ Zip _____

— —

FAT FREE LIVING 3 Desserts

15202 North 50th Place • Scottsdale, Arizona 85254 • (602) 996-6300

Please send me _____ copies of your cookbook at $15.95 each plus $4.00 for postage , sales tax, and handling. Enclosed is my check payable to FAT FREE LIVING for $_____.

Name _____

Address _____

City _____ State _____ Zip _____

— —

FAT FREE LIVING 4 Breads

15202 North 50th Place • Scottsdale, Arizona 85254 • (602) 996-6300

Please send me _____ copies of your cookbook at $14.95 each plus $5.00 for postage , sales tax, and handling. Enclosed is my check payable to FAT FREE LIVING for $_____.

Name _____

Address _____

City _____ State _____ Zip _____

— —

MORE FAT FREE RECIPES

Share your fat-free recipes with the rest of the world!
If you have a fat-free recipe that you feel belongs in
Recipes for FAT FREE LIVING 4, please send it to me.

> Jyl Steinback
> Recipes for FAT FREE LIVING
> 15202 North 50th Place
> Scottsdale, Arizona 85254
> (602) 996-6300

We will make sure that you get credited for your
contribution with your name appearing on the page
with your recipe. You will also receive a free copy of
Recipe for FAT FREE LIVING 4 when published.

So please state your name, address and telephone
number, with your signature under your recipe.

You may also contact me at the above address for
speaking engagements or information about FAT FREE
LIVING, INC.

Love you lots,

And thanks for all your positive feedback! I appreciate
YOU!

Jyl Steinback

RESULTS!

FAT-FREE COOKBOOK + VIDEO = RESULTS

SOON TO BE RELEASED

JYL STEINBACK'S EXERCISE VIDEO

FEATURING <u>NEW</u> RESISTANT BANDS

40-MINUTE BODY SCULPTING WORKOUT
(stretch & tone)

IT'S NEW! IT'S HOT! IT WORKS!!
Send now for information

_____

Name _____

Address _____

City _____ State _____ Zip _____

Jyl Steinback
FAT FREE LIVING, INC.
15202 North 50th Place
Scottsdale, Arizona 85254

Index

Angel Food Cake Trifle 219
Apple-Cinnamon Puffy Pancake 60
Apple-Cinnamon Raisin Bread Pudding 59
Apple Crisp 215
Apple Honey Cake 216
Apple Pudding 227
Artichoke Casserole 195
Artichoke Dip 4
Artichoke Heart Spread 19
Artichoke Pita Chips 26
Asparagus Dijon 196
"Au Gratin" Potatoes 179
Au Gratin Potatoes 270
Baked Apples 279
Baked Fruit Compote 208
Baked Potato Chips 170
Baked Sole 132
Baked Ziti 154
Banana Berry Sandwich 65
Banana Shake 232
Bean and Cabbage Soup 33
Berry Delight 214
Black Bean Chili 31
Black Bean Dip 10
Black Bean Soup 40
Black and White Cheesecake 199
Blueberry Banana Shake 231
Blueberry Pancakes 61
Breakfast Burrito 55
Broccoli-Carrot Salad 74
Broccoli-Cauliflower Frittata 51
Broccoli-Cheese Casserole 152
Broccoli with Orange Sauce 198
Carrot Tzimmis 162
Cauliflower Pudding 163

Cheddar Macaroni Loaf...121
Cheese, Broccoli and Corn Casserole 120
Cheese Enchiladas 114
Cheese Toast..67
Cheesy Cauliflower 271
Cheese Crab Crisps 240
Cheesy Manicotti 268
Cheesy Seafood Potatoes 182
Cherry Vanilla Custard Cake 220
Chicken-Flavored Vegetable Soup................................37
Chili Potatoes 181
Chili Queso Bean Dip 243
Chili Relleno Casserole...57
Chili Rice..157
Chili Tortillas 115
Chilled Strawberry Soup 34
Chinese Vegetables with Pasta 146
Chocolate Meringues 228
Chocolate Pudding..278
Cinnamon Bialy Chips..68
Cod Fillets..134
Cold Pasta Primavera 156
Confetti Corn Frittata..53
Corn Pudding 165
Crab and Vegetable Salad 71
Crab Cakes...130
Crab Delight 127
Crab Devils 27
Crabmeat Dip 8
Crabmeat Dip with Zip 1
Crabmeat Soufflé 113
Cranberry Sauce 256
Cream of Broccoli Soup 254
Cream of Vegetable Soup 30
Creamy Caesar Dressing 102
Creamy Cole Slaw 96
Creamy Garlic Salad Dressing.....................................103

Creamy Jalapeño Dressing 108
Creamy Mashed Potatoes 174
Creamy Noodle Casserole 269
Creamy Parmesan Dressing 105
Creamy Salsa 16
Creamy Scrambled Eggs 249
Creamy Spinach Lasagna 145
Creole Fish with Rice 265
Crunchy-Munchy Vegetable Rounds 241
Crustless Pumpkin Pie 280
Crustless Spinach Quiche 54
Crustless Vegetable Pie 119
Curry Dip 6
Delectable Fish Fillets 141
Dessert Prunes 204
Dr. Rick's Crab Appetizer Recipe 21
Dr. Rick's Cucumber Salad 84
Egg Salad Sandwiches 45
Eggplant Casserole 123
Eggplant Pasta 110
Eggplant, Tomato, and Pepper Pasta 148
Eggplant Yogurt Dip 244
Elegant Cold Veggie Platter 20
Fabulous Flounder 137
Fat-Free Fabulous Carmel Apples 229
Fat-Free Fettuccini Alfredo 143
Fat-Free French Bread 48
Fat-Free Matzo Balls 36
Fat-Free Stuffing 194
Fat-Free Thousand Island Dressing 107
Fish Kabobs 263
Fish Parmesan 139
French Onion Soup 39
French Toast 247
Fresh Strawberry-Banana Sorbet 206
"Fried" Fillets 259
"Fried" Fish 262

Fried Scallops 129
Fruit and Cabbage Slaw 95
Fruit Delight 213
Fruit with Carmel Sauce 209
Fruit Yogurt Frozen Salad 221
Fruited Cottage Cheese 100
Fruity Bialy Snacks 252
Fruity Frozen Pops 210
Garlic Bread 49
Gazpacho Salad 78
Gazpacho Soup 38
Grilled Hoagie Sandwiches 46
Grilled Potatoes with Onions 184
Grilled Vegetable Medley 192
Happy Hour Crab Cocktail 264
Heavenly Angel Food Cake 217
Herb and Shrimp Spread 18
Holiday Fruit Compote 274
Honey-Cheese Crepes.......................................23
Honey-Loupe Freezer Sorbet 203
Honey-Mustard Dip...7
Honey-Mustard Potato Salad 79
Honey-Yogurt Dressing 106
Honey-Yogurt Fruit Salad 89
Hot and Healthy Breakfast Cereal 251
Hot and Spicy Tomato Salsa 14
Hot Bean Dip...9
Hot Crab Dip 239
Hot Potato Soup..253
Hot Spinach Salad 77
Huevos Rancheros...248
Italian Cod 136
Italian Coleslaw 94
Italian Spaghetti Squash 188
Lemon Cheesecake with Berry Topping 201
Lentil Rice 159
Light and Luscious Frozen Dessert 202

Marinated Tomato Salad 82
Marinated Veggies 272
Meatless Chili Bean Tortillas 116
Melon Melba 205
Mexican Chili-Bean Coleslaw 97
Mexican Lasagna 150
Mexican Layer Dip 12
Mexican Rice 158
Minestrone Soup..35
Molded Gazpacho Salad 76
Mushroom-Barley Soup 41
Mushroom-Cheese Sandwich 43
Mushroom Deluxe..167
Nacho Cheese Dip 13
Nine Layer Salad 87
Oatmeal Pancakes 62
Onion Cheese Puffs 24
Onion Spread 17
Orange-Cheese Spread Sandwiches 64
Orange French Toast 63
Orange Jello Mold 90
Oriental Fat-Free Turkey Salad 86
Oriental Pasta 155
Outrageous Caesar Salad 83
Oven Baked Seafood Salad 112
Parmesan-Vegetable Salad 72
Pasta Con Broccoli 144
Pasta Genovese 153
Pasta Salad with a Twist..99
Pasta Shells Florentine 149
Pasta with Mushrooms 147
Peach-Banana Bread Pudding 224
Pepper Cheese Dip 3
Pineapple Cheesecake..200
Pineapple Sandwiches 212
Pineapple Shrimp 140
Pineapple Slaw...92

Pineapple Sweet Potatoes 171
Pineapple-Tangerine Refresher 237
Plum Creme..223
Polynesian Bread Pudding...276
Potato Boats 168
Potato Casserole 176
Potato Fans 186
Potato Kugel 173
Potato Latkes 180
Potato Salad 88
Potato Salad with Pizzazz 98
Pretzels 47
Pumpkin Pudding 275
Quesadillas 242
Quesadillas with Vegetable Fillings 15
Quick Peach Papaya Fizz 236
Quick Pudding Parfaits 225
Raspberry Mint Tea...234
Raspberry-Peach Iced Tea 235
Raspberry Sorbet 207
Ratatouille...273
Rice Pudding 226
Roasted Potatoes with Red Peppers 185
Salad Dressing 101
"Sauteed" Zucchini 191
Scallops Parmesan 128
Scrumptious Mashed Potatoes 178
Seafood Rice Casserole 109
Seafood Rice Casserole 266
Seafood Stuffed Fish 135
Shrimp and Greens 131
Shrimp Dip 246
Shrimp Primavera 133
Shrimp Scramble 111
Simply Divine Sole 258
Southwest Fillet of Sole 138
Spicy Green Chile Dressing 104

Spicy Vegetables 193
Spinach-Cheese Bake 56
Spinach Dip 5
Spinach Dip, in Loaf 245
Spinach Rice Ring 187
Spinach Stuffed Sole...261
Spring Garden Salad 80
Strawberry-Banana Bread 66
Strawberry Mousse 277
Strawberry-Orange Shortcake 218
Strawberry Shake 233
Strawberry Surprise Jello Mold 91
Stuffed Mushrooms...25
Stuffed Tomatoes 189
Summer Veggie Salad 85
Super Seafood Salad Sandwich 44
Super Stuffed Potatoes...177
Sweet-and-Sour Beans 197
Sweet and Sour Fish Fillets 260
Sweet and Sour Red Cabbage 161
Sweet and Tangy Sweet Potatoes 183
Sweet and Sour Salad..75
Sweet and Sour Sauce 255
Sweet Cinnamon Raisin Spread 69
Sweet Pepper Slaw 93
Sweet Potato Casserole 172
Swiss Cheese Tomato Bake 122
Tangy Green Beans 166
Tangy Mustard Cauliflower 164
Teriyaki Vegetables with Rice 267
Tomato-Fish Pasta Sauce 142
Tomato Pasta Sauce 73
Trifle Fruit Salad 222
Tuna Chowder 29
Tuna Rice Casserole 125
Twice-Baked Potatoes, Cottage Style 175
Two-Time Potatoes 169

"Unfried" Fried Zucchini and Mushrooms 22
Vegetable Burrito Casserole 117
Vegetable Casserole 124
Vegetable Dip..11
Vegetable Dip with Zip 2
Vegetable Frittata 52
Vegetable Potato Salad 81
Vegetable Soup 32
Vegetarian Lasagna 151
Veggie Bake 118
Veggie Burgers..126
Veggie Pita Pocket Sandwiches 42
Very Veggie Omelet 250
Yogurt Melon-Ring Supreme..211
Zucchini, Carrot and Onion Quiche 58
Zucchini Pancakes 190